Street Atlas of
TORBA

C000126385

Key to Maps

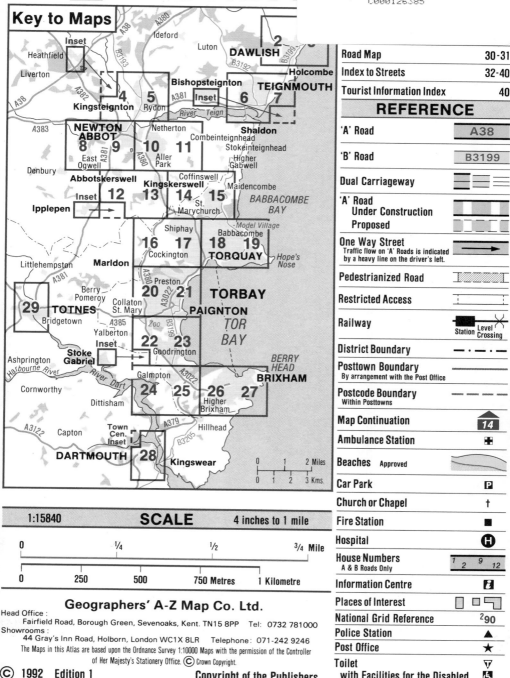

Road Map	30-31
Index to Streets	32-40
Tourist Information Index	40

REFERENCE

'A' Road	A38
'B' Road	B3199
Dual Carriageway	
'A' Road Under Construction Proposed	
One Way Street Traffic flow on 'A' Roads is indicated by a heavy line on the driver's left.	→
Pedestrianized Road	
Restricted Access	
Railway	Station / Level Crossing
District Boundary	— · — · —
Posttown Boundary By arrangement with the Post Office	
Postcode Boundary Within Posttowns	
Map Continuation	14
Ambulance Station	
Beaches Approved	
Car Park	P
Church or Chapel	†
Fire Station	■
Hospital	H
House Numbers A & B Roads Only	1 2 9 12
Information Centre	i
Places of Interest	
National Grid Reference	290
Police Station	▲
Post Office	★
Toilet with Facilities for the Disabled	▽

1:15840	**SCALE**	4 inches to 1 mile	

0	¼	½	¾ Mile

0	250	500	750 Metres	1 Kilometre

Geographers' A-Z Map Co. Ltd.

Head Office :
Fairfield Road, Borough Green, Sevenoaks, Kent. TN15 8PP   Tel: 0732 781000
Showrooms :
44 Gray's Inn Road, Holborn, London WC1X 8LR   Telephone: 071-242 9246
The Maps in this Atlas are based upon the Ordnance Survey 1:10000 Maps with the permission of the Controller of Her Majesty's Stationery Office. © Crown Copyright.

© 1992   Edition 1   Copyright of the Publishers

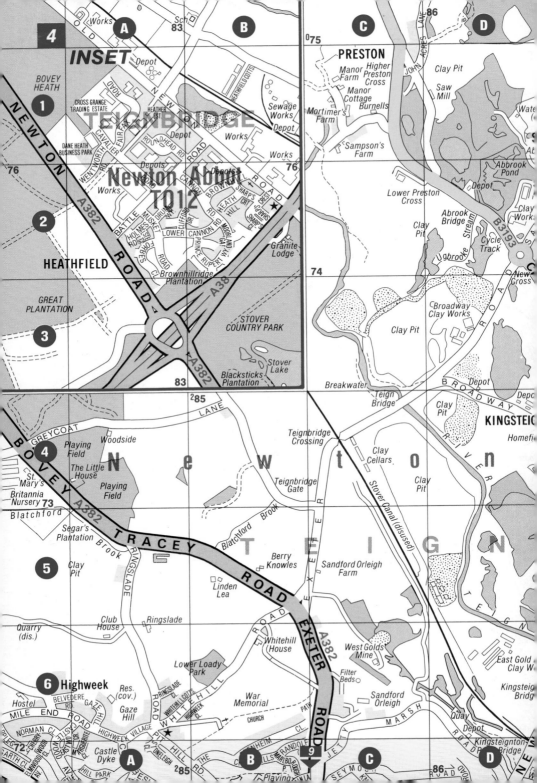

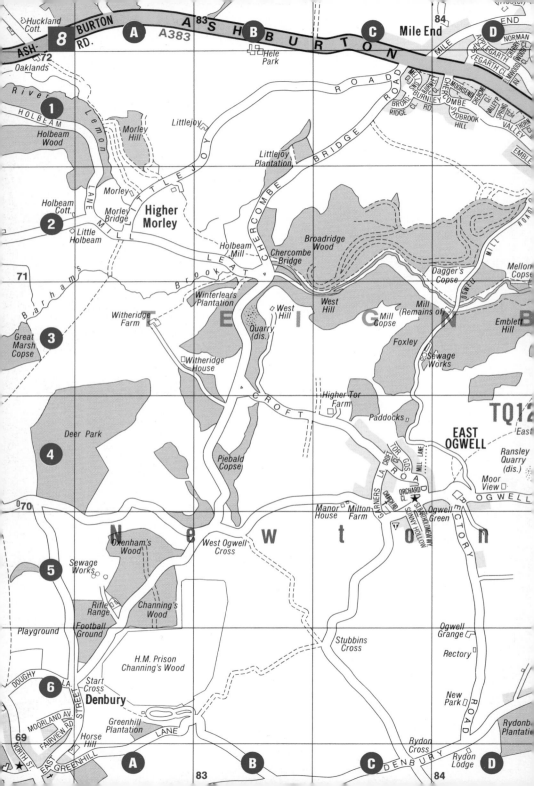

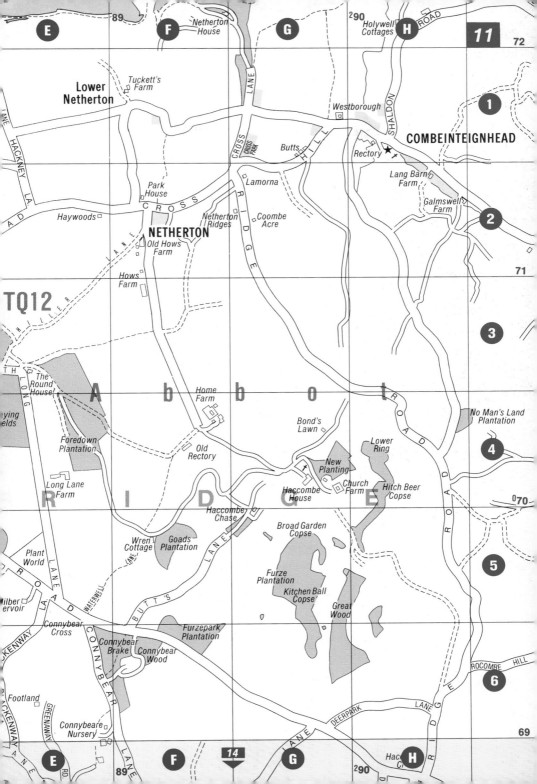

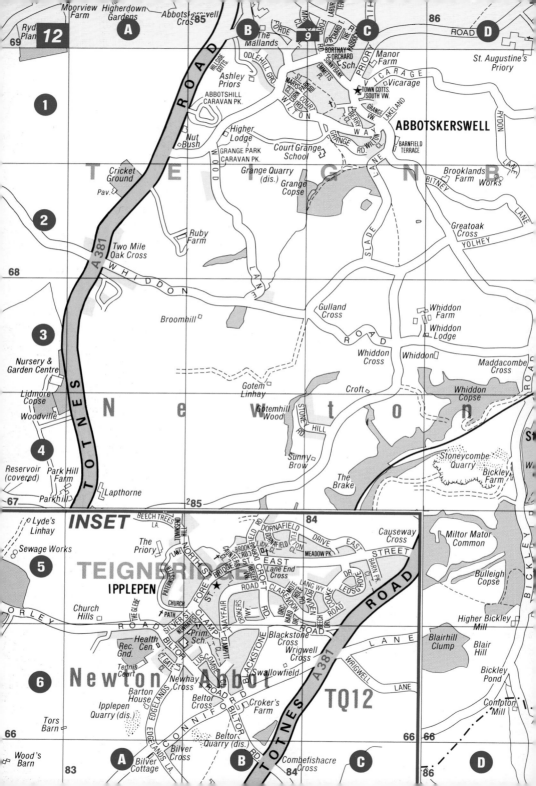

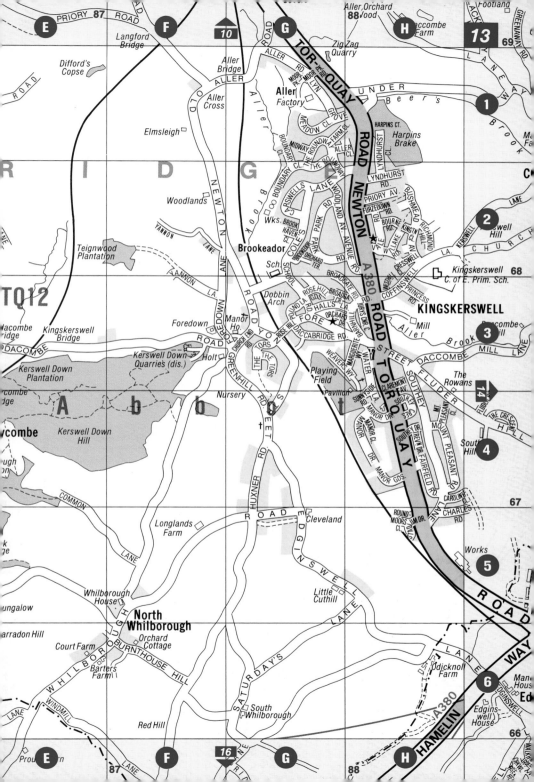

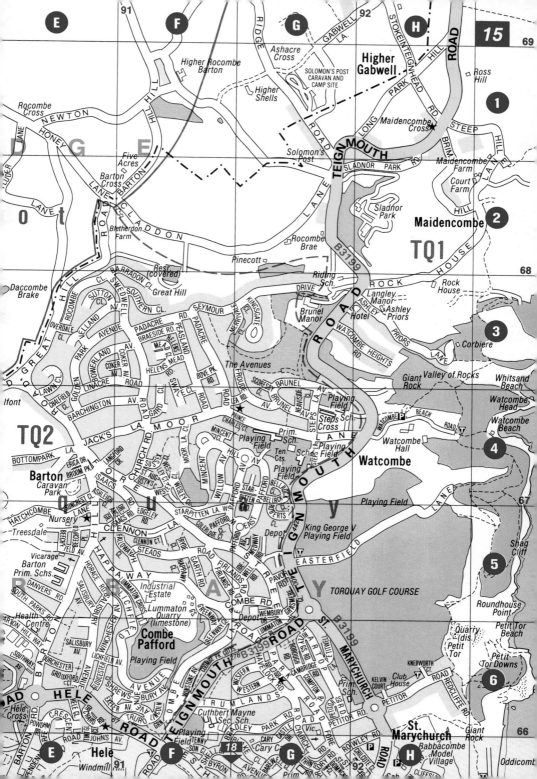

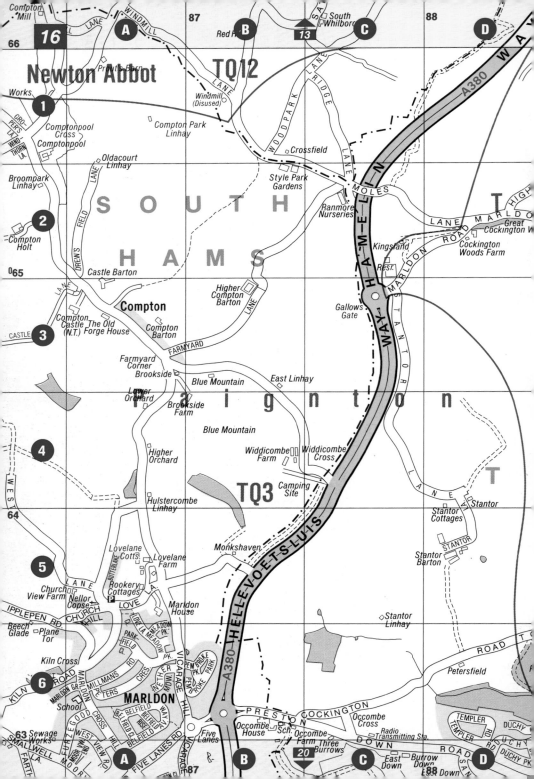

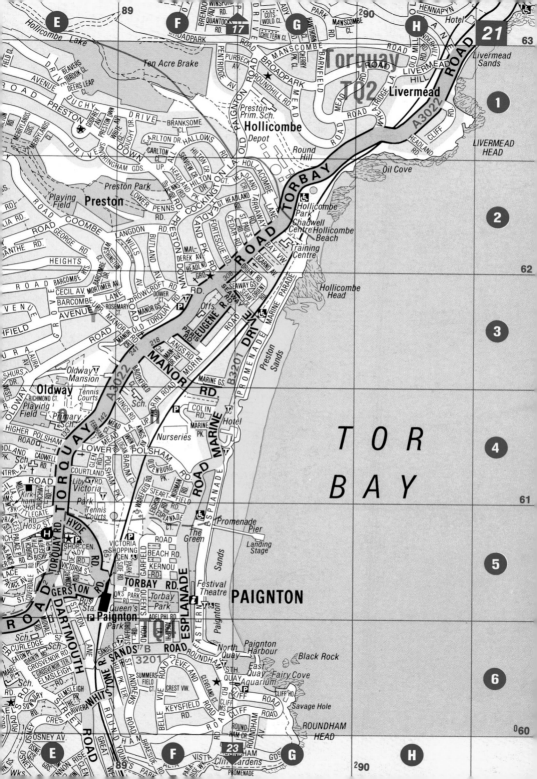

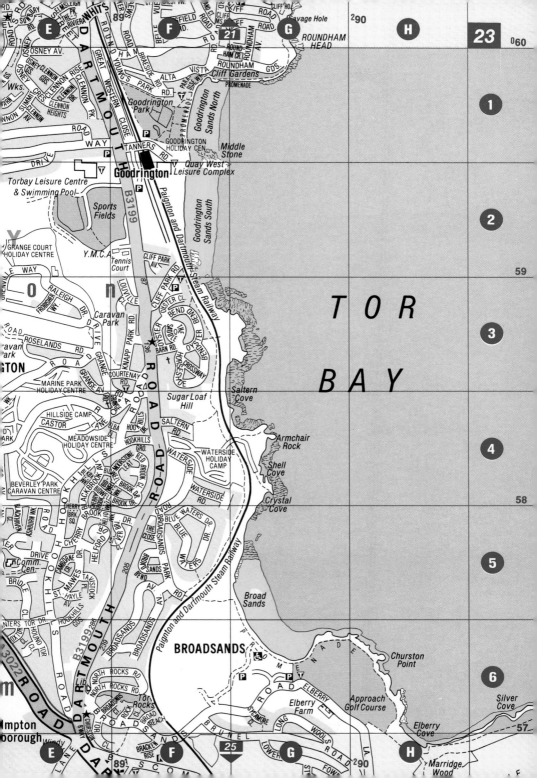

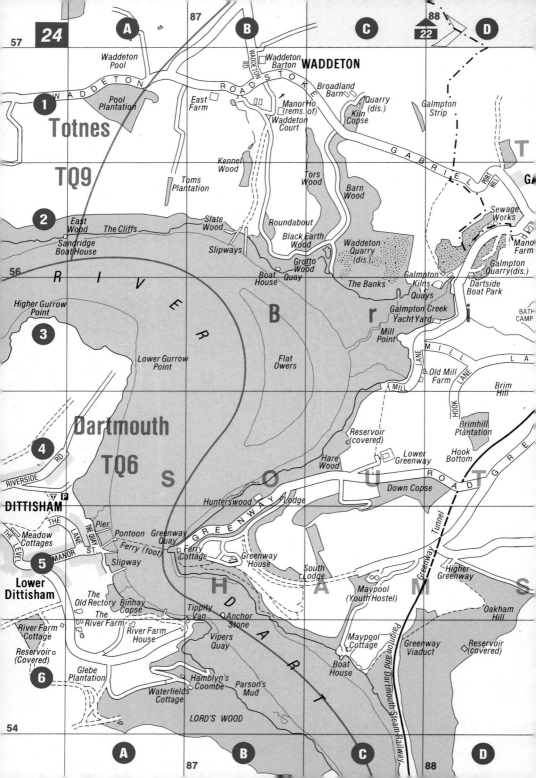

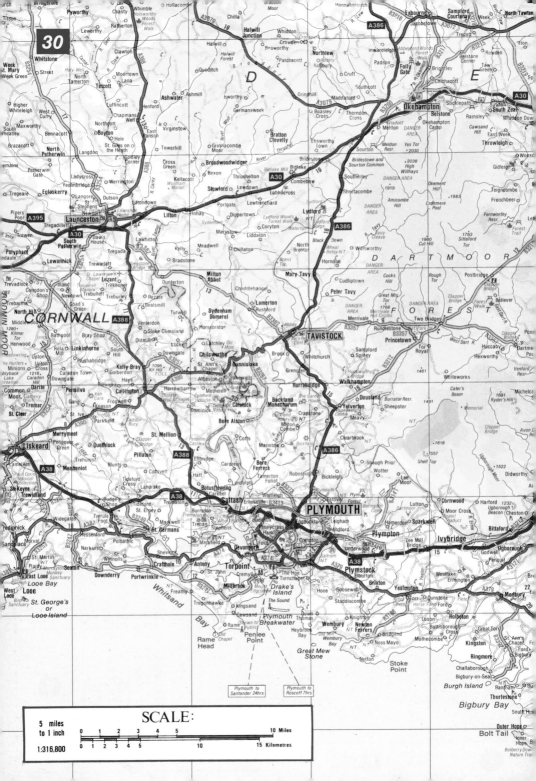

TOURIST INFORMATION

AIRPORT, INTERNATIONAL		LIGHTHOUSE	
AIRFIELD		MOTOR RACING CIRCUIT	
HELIPORT		MUSEUM	
BATTLE SITE & DATE	1066	NATIONAL & FOREST PARK	
CASTLE		NATIONAL TRUST PROPERTY (Open)	NT
CASTLE WITH GARDEN (Open to Public)		(Restricted Opening)	NT
CATHEDRAL, ABBEY, PRIORY etc.		NATURE RESERVE & BIRD SANCTUARY	
COUNTRY PARK		NATURE TRAIL & FOREST WALK	
FERRY (VEHICULAR)		PLACE OF INTEREST	
(FOOT ONLY)		PICNIC SITE	
GARDEN (Open to Public)		RAILWAY, STEAM or NARROW GAUGE	
GOLF COURSE 9. 18.		TELEPHONE, PUBLIC (Selection) ... AA or RAC	
HISTORIC BUILDING (Open to Public)		VIEW POINT	
HISTORIC BUILDING WITH GARDEN(Open to Public)		WILDLIFE PARK	
HORSE RACECOURSE		WINDMILL	
INFORMATION CENTRE		ZOO or SAFARI PARK	

Torquay to Alderney 5hrs. 35mins.
Torquay to Guernsey 6hrs.
Torquay to Jersey 9hrs 15mins.
(Summer Only)

HOW TO USE THIS INDEX

1. Each name is followed by its Postcode District and then by its map reference, e.g. Abbey Rd. TQ2—4B 18 is in the TQ2 Postcode District and appears in map square 4B on Page 18. It is not recommended that this index be used as a means of addressing mail.

2. A strict alphabetical order is followed in which Avenue, Road, Street etc., (even though abbreviated) are read as part of the name preceding them e.g. Ashridge Gdns. appears after Ash Pk. but before Ash Rd.

3. Street and subsidiary names not shown on the Maps, appear in *Italics* with the thoroughfare to which it is connected shown in brackets.

GENERAL ABBREVIATIONS

All : Alley	Cir : Circus	Gt : Great	M : Mews	Sta : Station
App : Approach	Clo : Close	Grn : Green	Mt : Mount	St : Street
Arc : Arcade	Comn : Common	Gro : Grove	N : North	Ter : Terrace
Av : Avenue	Cotts : Cottages	Ho : House	Pal : Palace	Up : Upper
Bk : Back	Ct : Court	Ind : Industrial	Pde : Parade	Vs : Villas
Boulevd : Boulevard	Cres : Crescent	Junct : Junction	Pk : Park	Wlk : Walk
Bri : Bridge	Dri : Drive	La : Lane	Pas : Passage	W : West
B'way : Broadway	E : East	Lit : Little	Pl : Place	Yd : Yard
Bldgs : Buildings	Embkmt : Embankment	Lwr : Lower	Rd : Road	
Chu : Church	Est : Estate	Mnr : Manor	S : South	
Chyd : Churchyard	Gdns : Gardens	Mans : Mansions	Sq : Square	
Circ : Circle	Ga : Gate	Mkt : Market	St : Street	

INDEX TO STREETS

Abbey Rd. TQ2—4B 18
Abbotsbury Rd. TQ12—1G 9
Abbotshill Caravan Pk. TQ12
  —1B 12
Abbotsridge Dri. TQ12—4E 9
Abbotswell Cotts.
  TQ12—6G 9
  (off Ford Rd.)
Abbrook Av. TQ12—2E 5
Above Town. TQ6—2A 28
  & 4C 28
Acacia Clo. TQ12—6F 5
Acadia Rd. TQ1—5F 19
Acre La. TQ1—3F 19
Addison Rd. TQ4—6D 20
Addison Rd. TQ12—4B 10
Adelphi La. TQ4—6F 21
Adelphi Rd. TQ4—5F 21
Admirals Wlk. TQ14—1C 6
Ailescombe Dri. TQ3—5C 20
Ailescombe Rd. TQ3—4C 20
Aish Rd. TQ9—5A 22
Alandale Clo. TQ14—3E 7
Alandale Rd. TQ14—3E 7
Albany Rd. TQ3—1D 20
Albany St. TQ12—2H 9
Alberta Ct. TQ14—4E 7
  (off Myrtle Hill)
Albert Pl. TQ6—1A 28
Albert Rd. TQ1—4C 18
Albert St. EX7—4D 2
Albert Ter. TQ12—2H 9
Albion Hill. TQ12—3H 9
Albion St. TQ14—6C 6
Alder Clo. TQ12—5C 10
Alders Way. TQ4—2A 22
Alexandra Ho. TQ12—3B 10
Alexandra La. TQ1—4C 18
Alexandra Rd. EX7—4D 2
Alexandra Rd. TQ1—3C 18
Alexandra Rd. TQ12—3A 10
Alexandra Ter. TQ9—3F 29
Alexandra Ter. TQ12—3H 9
Alexandra Ter. TQ14—5D 6
Alison Rd. TQ3—2D 20
Aller Brake Rd. TQ12—5B 10
Aller Clo. TQ12—1G 13
Aller Hill. EX7—5B 2
Aller Pk. Rd. TQ12—5B 10
Aller Rd. TQ12—1F 13
All Hallows Rd. TQ3—1F 21
All Saints Rd. TQ1—3D 18
Alma Rd. TQ5—2D 26
Alpha Ter. TQ9—3E 29
Alpine Rd. TQ1—4C 18
Alston La. TQ5—5F 25
Alta Vista Clo. TQ14—2F 7

Alta Vista Rd. TQ4—1F 23
Alwyns Clo. TQ14
  —4E 7
  (off Lwr. Brimley)
Andor Av. TQ12—4E 5
Ansteys Clo. TQ1—4F 19
Anstey's Cove Rd. TQ1—3F 19
Anthea Rd. TQ3—2C 20
Antrim Ter. TQ9—3F 29
Anzac St. TQ6—1A 28 & 4C 28
Applegarth Av. TQ12—2E 5
Applegarth Clo. TQ12—1D 8
Apters Hill. TQ5—2D 26
  (off Middle St.)
Arch Cotts. TQ12—4E 5
Arch St. TQ14—6C 6
Archway Dri. TQ6—3A 28
Arden Dri. TQ2—3G 17
Argyle Ter. TQ9—3E 29
  (off Station Rd.)
Armada Cres. TQ2—3F 17
Armada Dri. TQ14—1C 6
Arthington. TQ1—2A 18
Ashburn Wlk. TQ4—5E 23
Ashburton Rd. TQ9—2E 29
Ashburton Rd. TQ12—1B 8
Ashcombe Rd. EX7—1A 2
Asheldon Rd. TQ1—4F 19
Ashfield Clo. TQ12—5H 17
Ashfield Rd. TQ2—4H 17
Ash Hill. TQ14—5H 7
Ash Hill Rd. TQ1—3B 18
Ashleigh Clo. TQ2—4E 15
Ashleigh Clo. TQ14—2D 6
Ashleigh La. TQ1—6E 19
Ashleigh Dri. TQ14—2D 6
Ashleigh Gdns. TQ6—3A 28
Ashleigh Mt. TQ14—2D 6
Ashleigh Pk. TQ14—2D 6
Ashleigh Rise. TQ14—2D 6
Ashleigh Way. TQ14—2D 6
Ashley Priors La. TQ1—3H 15
Ashley Way. TQ3—3F 3
Ashridge Gdns. TQ12—6G 5
Ash Pk. EX7—1G 7
Ash Rd. TQ12—5F 5
Ashton Ct. TQ12—2F 5
Ashton Ter. TQ1—4F 19
Ash Way. TQ12—4C 10
Aspen Dri. TQ12—5C 10
Aspen Way. TQ4—2A 22
Audley Av. TQ12—4C 10
Audley Rise. TQ12—4D 10
Aveland Rd. TQ1—2D 18
Avenue Rd. TQ3—3H 17
Avenue Rd. TQ12—2H 13
Avenue, The. TQ1—1A 10

Avoca Av. TQ1—3A 18
Avon Rd. TQ2—2E 17

Babbacombe Downs Rd. TQ1
  —1D 18
Babbacombe Rd. TQ1—1D 18
Babbage Rd. TQ9—3F 29
Back Rd. TQ12—2F 5
Badgers Clo. TQ12—3E 5
Badlake Hill. EX7—3C 2
Bakers Hill. TQ5—4D 26
Bakers Hill. TQ12—2G 9
Bakers View. TQ12—2F 9
Bala Brook Clo. TQ5—5A 26
Balmoral Clo. TQ12—3B 10
Bampfylde Rd. TQ2—4A 18
Bampton Clo. TQ3—1A 20
Banbury Pk. TQ2—1F 17
Bank La. TQ5—2D 26
  (off Union La.)
Bank La. TQ9—4F 29
  (off Fore St.)
Bank St. TQ12—2G 9
Bank St. TQ14—5E 7
Barchington Av. TQ2—4E 15
Barcombe Dri. TQ3—3E 21
Barcombe Heights. TQ3—3D 20
Barcombe La. TQ3—3E 21
Barcombe Rd. TQ3—3D 20
Barewell Clo. TQ1—1C 18
Barewell Rd. TQ1—1C 18
Barn Ct. TQ5—3H 25
Barnfield Clo. TQ5—2F 25
Barnfield Rd. TQ2—1G 21
Barnfield Rd. TQ3—4C 20
Barnfield Rd. TQ4—4E 27
Barnfield Ter. TQ5—2H 25
Barnfield Ter. TQ12—1C 12
Barnhill Rd. TQ12—3H 13
Barn Pk. TQ9—5A 22
Barn Pk. Clo. TQ12—5C 12
Barnpark Clo. TQ14—4E 7
Barnpark Rd. TQ14—4E 7
Barnpark Ter. TQ14—3E 7
Barn Rd. TQ4—3F 23
Barns Clo. TQ12—5F 5
Barnsley Clo. TQ14—4E 7
Barnsley Dri. TQ14—4E 7
Barracks Hill. TQ9—3E 29
Barradon Clo. TQ2—3F 15
Barrington Rd. TQ1—4F 19
Barton Av. TQ3—5C 20
Barton Clo. TQ3—4C 20
Barton Cres. EX7—4C 2
Barton Cres. TQ3—4C 20
Barton Dri. TQ3—4C 20

Barton Dri. TQ12—2E 9
Barton Gdns. TQ3—4C 20
Barton Hall Caravan and Chalet
  Cen. TQ2—4D 14
Barton Hill. EX7—4C 2
Barton Hill. TQ12—2F 15
Barton Hill Rd. TQ2—6E 15
Barton Hill Way. TQ2—6E 15
Barton La. EX7—4D 2
Barton Rd. TQ2 & TQ1—1H 17
Barton Rd. TQ3—4C 20
Barton Ter. EX7—4D 2
Barton Vs. EX7—4D 2
Barum Clo. TQ3—4F 21
Bascombe Clo. TQ5—1G 25
Bascombe Rd. TQ5—1F 25
Bathill Camp Site. TQ5—3D 24
Bath La. TQ2—4A 18
Bath Ter. TQ14—5E 7
Batson Gdns. TQ4—1E 23
Battersway Rd. TQ4—1B 22
Battle Rd. TQ12—2A 4
Baymount. TQ3—4D 20
Bay View. TQ3—2G 21
Bay View Dri. TQ14—3E 7
Beach App. Footpath.
  TQ5—2E 27
  (off Pump St.)
Beach Rd. EX7—1H 3
Beach Rd. TQ1—2E 19
Beach Rd. TQ4—5F 21
Beach St. EX7—4E 3
Beacon Hill. TQ1—6C 18
Beacon La. TQ6—5D 28
Beacon Rd. TQ6—5D 28
Beaumont Clo. TQ2—3G 17
Beaumont Rd. TQ12—3H 9
Beavers Brook Clo. TQ3—1E 21
Bedford Rd. TQ1—1E 19
Beech Dri. TQ12—5C 12
Beechfield Av. TQ2—5E 15
Beechfield Pl. TQ2—5E 15
Beech Trees La. TQ12—5A 12
Beechwood Av. TQ12—4B 10
Beechwood Ct. TQ14—2B 6
Beenland Gdns. TQ2
  —3A 18
  (off East St.)
Beenland Pl. TQ2
  —3A 18
  (off East St.)
Belfield Av. TQ3—1A 20
Belfield Clo. TQ3—6A 16
Belfield Rise. TQ3—6A 16
Belfield Rd. TQ3—4B 20

Belfield Way. TQ3—6A 16
Belgrave Rd. TQ2—4A 18
Belgrave Rd. TQ12—4C 10
Belgrave Ter. TQ1—4E 7
Bella Vista Rd. TQ5—1D 26
Bellever Tor Dri. TQ5—5A 26
Belle Vue Rd. TQ4—6F 21
Bellrock Clo. TQ2—4G 15
Belmont Clo. TQ12—2F 5
Belmont Rd. TQ1—3C 18
Belmont Rd. TQ5—3D 26
Belmont Ter. TQ9—3F 29
Belvedere Rd. TQ12—6A 4
Bench Tor Clo. TQ2—1E 17
Ben Jonson Clo. TQ2—3G 17
Ben Venue Clo. TQ1—4D 18
Berachah Rd. TQ1—3C 18
Berea Rd. TQ1—3D 18
Bere Cotts. EX7—3B 2
Bere Hill. EX7—4B 2
Berkeley Av. TQ2—6B 14
Berkeley Rise. TQ2—6B 14
Berry Av. TQ3—5C 20
Berry Clo. TQ12—1C 12
Berry Ct. TQ5—1F 27
Berry Dri. TQ3—5C 20
Berry Head Rd. TQ5—2E 27
Berry Hill. TQ14—5G 7
Berry La. TQ12—4F 5
Berry Rd. TQ3—5C 20
Berry Sq. TQ4—5F 21
  (off Beach Rd.)
Berrys Wood. TQ12—2E 9
Besigheim Way. TQ12—2B 10
Beverley Pk. Caravan Cen. TQ4
  —4E 23
Beverley Rise. TQ5—3C 26
Beverley Way. TQ12—3F 9
Bexley La. TQ4—4A 18
Bickford La. TQ14—5E 7
Bickley Rd. TQ12—5D 12
Bidwell Brook Dri. TQ4—4E 23
Bidwell Wlk. TQ4—4E 23
Biltor Rd. TQ12—6A 12
Bingfield Clo. TQ1—4D 18
Birch Rd. TQ12—4C 10
Birch Wlk. TQ12—1F 17
Birdwood Ct. TQ9—4F 29
Bishops Av. TQ14—6G 7
Bishops Clo. TQ1—5G 19
Bishops Ct. TQ14—5G 7
Bishop's Pl. TQ3—5E 21
Bishops Rise. TQ1—5H 19
Bishopsteignton Rd. TQ14
  —5A 6
Bishop's Wlk. TQ1—3G 19

Bishop Wilfrid Rd. TQ14—3B 6
Bitney La. TQ12—2D 12
Bitton Av. TQ14—4D 6
Bitton Pk. Rd. TQ14—4C 6
(in two parts)
Blackball La. TQ5—1D 26
Blackbrook Av. TQ4—4E 23
Blackbrook Wlk. TQ4—4E 23
Blackenway La. TQ12—6E 11
Blackhaven Clo. TQ4—5E 23
Blackpost La. TQ9—4H 29
Blackstone. TQ2—1C 18
Blackthorn Way. TQ4—1A 22
Blagdon Rd. TQ3—6A 20
Blake Clo. TQ1—1C 18
Blakey Down La. TQ3—2B 20
Blatchcombe Dri. TQ3—4C 20
Blatchcombe Rd. TQ3—4C 20
Blenheim Clo. TQ1—5F 19
Blenheim Clo. TQ12—1F 9
Bligh Clo. TQ1—1C 6
Blindwell Av. TQ12—4F 5
Blindwylle Rd. TQ2—4H 17
Blue Ball Hill. TQ9—4F 29
Blue Waters Dri. TQ4—5F 23
Blyths Wood Cres. TQ1—2C 18
Body Hayes Clo. TQ9—6A 22
Bolton St. TQ3—3D 26
Bonair Clo. TQ5—4D 26
Borough Clo. TQ4—2B 22
Borough Pk. Rd. TQ3—6A 20
Borough Rd. TQ3—3F 29
Borough Rd. TQ1—6G 15
Borough Rd. TQ4—1A 22
Borthay Orchard. TQ12—1C 12
Boscawen Ct. TQ1—4D 6
Bottompark La. TQ4—4E 15
Bottoms La. TQ12—3D 14
Boundary Clo. TQ12—1G 13
Boundary Rd. TQ2—4G 17
Bourne Ct. TQ5—5A 26
Bourne Rd. TQ12—2H 13
Bourton La. TQ9—3H 29
Bourton Rd. TQ9—3H 29
Bove Pk. Rd. TQ2—3F 15
Bovey Tracey Rd. TQ12—4A 4
Bowden Hill. TQ12—3H 9
Bowden Rd. TQ12—5C 12
Bowerland Av. TQ2—3E 15
Bowland Clo. TQ4—3D 22
Boyds Dri. TQ14—4E 7
Bracken Rise. TQ4—1F 25
Bradden Cres. TQ5—3B 26
Braddons Cliffe. TQ1—5C 18
Braddons Hill Rd. E. TQ1
—5C 18
Braddons Hill Rd. W. TQ1
—5C 18
Braddons St. TQ1—5C 18
Bradley Ct. TQ12—2G 9
Bradley La. TQ12—2F 9
Bradley Pk. Rd. TQ1—1B 18
Bradley Rd. TQ12—4F 9
Braeside Rd. TQ2—3F 15
Braeside Rd. TQ4—1F 23
Brake Houses. TQ12
Brakeridge Clo. TQ5—1F 25
Bramble Clo. TQ2—6D 14
Branksome Clo. TQ3—1F 21
Branscombe Clo. TQ1—3E 19
Brantwood Clo. TQ4—1D 22
Brantwood Cres. TQ4—2D 22
Brantwood Dri. TQ4—1D 22
Breakneck Hill. TQ14—1D 6
Brendons Av. TQ2—6F 17
Brent Rd. TQ3—5E 21
Brewery La. TQ5
—2D 26
(off Market St.)
Briary La. TQ1—4C 18
Bridge Rd. TQ2—4A 18
Bridge Rd. TQ5—2G 25
Bridge Rd. TQ6—1D 28
Bridge Rd. TQ14—6C 6
Bridge St. TQ12—5B 12
Bridgetown. TQ9—4G 29
Bridgetown Hill. TQ9—4G 29
Bridgetown Hill TQ9—4G 29
Bridle Clo. TQ4—5E 23
Brim Brook Ct. TQ2
—1E 17
(off Chinkwell Rise)
Brim Hill. TQ1—1H 15
Brimlands. TQ5—3C 26
Brimley Dri. TQ14—4E 7

Briseham Clo. TQ5—5E 27
Briseham Rd. TQ5—4E 27
Britannia Av. TQ6—4A 28
Briwere Rd. TQ1—2H 17
Brixham Holiday Pk. TQ5
—1C 26
Brixham Rd. TQ4—1B 22
Brixham Rd. TQ6—4D 28
Broadacre Dri. TQ2—2E 27
Broadgate Rd. TQ12—2G 13
Broadlands. TQ14—6C 6
Broadlands Av. TQ2—2F 9
Broadlands Ct. TQ12—2F 9
Broadlands Rd. TQ4—1D 22
Broadley Dri. TQ2—6F 17
Broadmeadow Ind. Est. TQ14
—4B 6
Broadmeadow La. TQ14—3A 6
Broadmeadow View. TQ14
—4B 6
Broad Pk. TQ6—4A 28
Broadpark Rd. TQ2—6F 17
Broadpark Rd. TQ3—3C 20
Broad Path. TQ9—4E 29
Broad Reach. TQ4—6F 23
Broadridge Clo. TQ12—1C 8
Broadsands Av. TQ4—6F 23
Broadsands Bend. TQ4—6F 23
Broadsands Ct. TQ4—6E 23
Broadsands Pk. Rd. TQ4
—5F 23
Broadsands Rd. TQ4—6E 23
Broadstone. TQ6—1A 28
& 3C 28
Broadstone Pk. Rd. TQ2
—6G 17
Broadway Av. TQ12—3E 5
Broadway Rd. TQ12—3D 4
Bronescombe Av. TQ14—5H 7
Bronshill Rd. TQ1—3C 18
Brook Clo. EX7—1G 7
Brookdale Clo. TQ5—3C 26
Brookdale Pk. TQ5—3C 26
Brookdale Ter. EX7—4E 3
Brookfield Clo. TQ3—3F 21
Brookfield Rd. TQ3—2E 7
Brook Haven Clo. TQ12—2G 13
Brooklands. TQ9—5H 29
Brooklands La. TQ2—5H 17
Brook La. TQ14—6B 6
Brook Rd. TQ12—5B 12
Brookside Clo. TQ14—4C 6
Brook St. EX7—4D 2
Brookvale Clo. TQ14—6B 6
Brookvale Orchard. TQ14
—6B 6
Brook Way. TQ12—1F 5
Broom Clo. EX7—1F 3
Broomhill Way. TQ2—6D 14
Broom Pk. TQ2—4E 15
Brownhill. TQ2—2B 4
Brownhills Rd. TQ12—2F 9
Brownings End. TQ12—4E 9
Brownings Wlk. TQ12—4E 9
Brown's Hill. TQ6—1A 28
Brunel Av. TQ2—3G 15
Brunel Rd. TQ4—6F 23
Brunel Rd. TQ12—2A 10
Brunswick Pl. EX7—4D 2
Brunswick Sq. TQ1—3A 18
Brunswick St. TQ14—5E 7
Brunswick Ter. TQ1—3A 18
Buckeridge Av. TQ14—3D 6
Buckeridge Rd. TQ14—2D 6
Buckland Brake. TQ12—3B 10
Buckland Rd. TQ12—3B 10
(in three parts)
Buckland View. TQ12—1A 10
Budleigh Clo. TQ1—3E 19
Buller Rd. TQ12—3A 10
Bunting Clo. TQ12—4F 9
Burch Gdns. EX7—1E 3
Burdons Way. TQ12—1F 5
Burke Rd. TQ9—3G 29
Burleigh Rd. TQ2—2F 17
Burnley Clo. TQ12—1C 8
Burnley Rd. TQ12—1C 8
Burn River Rise. TQ2—1E 17
Burnthouse Hill. TQ12—6F 13
Burridge Av. TQ2—4G 17
Burridge La. TQ2—4B 18
Burridge Rd. TQ2—4G 17
Burton Pl. TQ5—3D 26

Burton St. TQ5—4D 26
Burton Villa Clo. TQ5—3D 26
Bury Rd. TQ12—1G 9
Bushell Rd. TQ12—1G 9
Bushmead Av. TQ12—2H 13
Butland Av. TQ3—2F 21
Butland Rd. TQ12—3E 5
Buttercombe Clo. TQ12—5E 9
Butterlake. TQ3—5A 16
Butt's La. TQ12—5F 11
Byron Rd. TQ1—1B 18
Byter Mill La. TQ9—6B 22

Cadewell Cres. TQ2—6C 14
Cadewell La. TQ2—1F 17
Cadewell Pk. Rd. TQ2—6B 14
Cadwell Rd. TQ4—4E 21
Calvados Pk. TQ12—3G 5
Camborne Cres. TQ4—5E 23
Cambridge Rd. TQ1—6G 15
Cambridge Rd. TQ5—3B 26
Camden Rd. TQ1—4C 18
Canal Way. TQ12—5E 5
Cannon Rd. TQ12—2B 4
Canons Clo. TQ14—5G 7
Captains Rd. TQ12—5C 12
Carew Gdns. TQ12—2C 10
Carey Rd. TQ6—4A 28
Carhaix Way. EX7—2F 3
Carlile Rd. TQ5—2B 26
Carlton Clo. TQ3—1F 21
Carlton Dri. TQ3—1F 21
Carlton Pl. TQ14—5E 7
Carlton Rd. TQ1—3D 18
Carlton Ter. EX7—4E 3
Caroline Clo. TQ12—4H 13
Carpenters Ct. TQ12
—3H 9
(off Church Rd.)
Carrions, The. TQ9—4F 29
Carswells. TQ12—2G 13
Cartwright Cres. TQ14—3B 6
Cary Av. TQ1—2C 18
Cary Castle Dri. TQ1—1C 18
Cary Pde. TQ2—5C 18
Cary Pk. Rd. TQ1—2D 18
Cary Rd. TQ2—5B 18
Cary Rd. TQ2—2D 20
Castle Cir. TQ1—4B 18
Castle Cir. Ct. TQ1—4B 18
Castle La. TQ1—4C 18
(in two parts)
Castle La. TQ3—3A 16
Castle Rd. TQ1—4C 18
Castle Rd. TQ6—6D 28
(Dartmouth)
Castle Rd. TQ6—5D 28
(Kingswear)
Castle St. TQ9—3F 29
Castle Way. TQ12—1D 8
Castlewood Av. TQ12—1D 8
Castor Clo. TQ5—4E 23
Castor La. TQ4—4E 23
Castor Rd. TQ5—4D 26
Caunters Clo. TQ12—5B 12
Cavalier Rd. TQ12—1A 4
Cavern Rd. TQ1—4C 18
Cavern Rd. TQ5—3D 26
Cecil Av. TQ3—3E 21
Cecilia Rd. TQ3—2D 20
Cecil Rd. TQ3—2F 21
Cedar Clo. TQ14—2F 7
Cedar Ct. Rd. TQ1—2C 18
Cedar Rd. TQ3—2F 21
Cedar Rd. TQ12—5C 10
Cedars Rd. TQ1—4D 18
Cedar Way. TQ5—5B 26
Central Av. TQ3—4E 21
Centry Ct. TQ5—3F 27
Centry Rd. TQ5—3F 27
Chalfield Clo. TQ2—4E 15
Challycroft Rd. TQ5—6B 26
Chapel Ct. TQ12—2A 18
Chapel La. TQ6—2A 28
Chapel Rd. TQ12—2A 10
Charlemont Rd. TQ14—1D 6
Charles Rd. TQ12—5H 13
Charles St. TQ6—1A 28 & 4C 28
Charmouth Clo. TQ1—3E 19
Chatsworth Rd. TQ1—3C 18
Chatto Rd. TQ1—2B 18
Chatto Way. TQ1—2B 18
Chelsea Pl. TQ14—4C 6

Chelston Rd. TQ2—6H 17
Chelston Rd. TQ2—1G 9
Chercombe Bri. Rd. TQ12—2B 8
Chercombe Clo. TQ12—1D 8
Chercombe Valley Rd. TQ12
—1D 8
Cherry Brook Dri. TQ4—5E 23
Cherry Brook Sq. TQ4—5E 23
Cherry Brook Wlk. TQ4—4E 23
Cherry Cross. TQ9—5F 29
Cherry Pk. Clo. TQ2—1G 21
Cherwood Clo. TQ12—1D 8
Chestnut Av. TQ2—5A 18
Chestnut Dri. TQ5—5A 26
Chestnut Dri. TQ12—5G 5
Chestnut Wlk. EX7—5C 2
Chichester Way. TQ12—2B 10
Chilcote Clo. TQ1—1D 18
Chiltern Clo. TQ2—6G 17
Chilton Av. TQ14—3E 7
Chinkwell Rise. TQ2—1E 17
Chiseldon Hill. TQ5—5D 26
Chockland Rd. TQ12—2E 5
Christina Pde. TQ9—4H 29
Christina Pk. TQ9—4H 29
Chudleigh Rd. TQ12—2F 5
Church Clo. TQ6—1B 28
& 4C 28
Church Clo. TQ9
—4F 29
(off High St. Totnes,)
Church End Rd. TQ12—3G 13
Churchfields Gdns. TQ6—4A 28
Churchfields W. TQ6—4A 28
Church Hill. TQ3—5A 16
Church Hill. TQ6—5D 28
Church Hill E. TQ5—2D 26
Church Hill W. TQ5—2D 26
Churchill Av. EX7—5D 2
Churchill Dri. TQ14—3E 7
Churchills, The. TQ12—1F 9
Church La. TQ2—4A 18
Church M. TQ12—5F 5
Church Path. TQ3—5E 21
Church Path. TQ12—5A 12
(Ipplepen)
Church Path. TQ12—6B 4
(Newton Abbot)
Church Rd. TQ1—6G 15
Church Rd. TQ2—4F 15
Church Rd. TQ12—4C 8
(East Ogwell)
Church Rd. TQ12—3H 9
(Newton Abbot)
Church Rd. TQ14—5H 7
Church St. EX7—4C 2
Church St. TQ2—4A 18
Church St. TQ3—5E 21
Church St. TQ5—2D 26
Church St. TQ12—5F 5
Church Wlk. TQ9—6A 22
Churchward Rd. TQ3—5E 21
Church Way. TQ1—2D 18
Church Way. TQ12—2A 14
(Kingskerswell)
Church Way. TQ12—4B 10
(Newton Abbot)
Churscombe Pk. TQ3—1A 20
Churscombe Rd. TQ3—1A 20
Churston B'way. TQ4—6E 23
Churston Clo. TQ5—2F 25
Churston Rd. TQ5—3H 25
Churston Way. TQ5—3B 26
Cistern St. TQ9—4E 29
Claddon La. TQ1—2F 15
Clampet La. TQ14
—5E 7
(off Bank St.)
Clampitt Clo. TQ12—6B 12
Clampitt Rd. TQ12—5B 12
Clanage St. TQ14—5G 7
Claremont Av. TQ12—3H 13
Clarence Hill. TQ6—1A 28
& 3C 28
Clarence St. TQ6—3C 28
Clarendon Clo. TQ1—2A 18
Clarendon Ct. TQ1—5D 18
Clarendon Rd. TQ12—5B 12
Clay La. TQ14—4D 6
Claypark Ter. TQ9—6B 22
Clennon Av. TQ4—1E 23
Clennon Ct. TQ4—1E 23
Clennon Dri. TQ4—1E 23
Clennon Gdns. TQ4—1E 23

Clennon Heights. TQ4—1E 23
Clennon La. TQ12—5F 15
Clennon La. TQ4—1D 22
Clennon Pk. TQ4—1E 23
Clennon Rise. TQ4—1E 23
Clennon Summit. TQ4—1E 23
Cleveland Ct. TQ4—6F 21
Cleveland Rise. TQ12—4E 9
Cleveland Rd. TQ2—3A 18
Cleveland Rd. TQ4—6F 21
Cliffden Clo. TQ14—4E 7
Cliff Ho. TQ4—6G 21
Cliff M. TQ4—6F 21
Clifford Av. TQ12—2E 5
Clifford Clo. TQ12—4F 5
Clifford Clo. TQ14—6C 6
Clifford Dri. TQ12—2A 4
Clifford St. TQ12—2E 5
Cliff Pk. Av. TQ4—2F 23
Cliff Pk. Rd. TQ4—3F 23
Cliff Rd. TQ12—1H 21
Cliff Rd. TQ4—6G 21
Cliff Rd. TQ14—2F 7
Cliffside Rd. TQ1—1D 18
Clifton Bank. TQ5—5D 20
Clifton Clo. TQ3—5C 20
Clifton Cres. TQ3—5D 20
Clifton Gdns. TQ3—5D 20
Clifton Gro. TQ3—5D 20
Clifton Pl. EX7—4C 2
Clifton Rise. TQ3—5D 20
Clifton Rd. TQ3—5C 20
Clifton Ter. TQ1—5C 18
Climsland Rd. TQ4—6D 20
Close, The. EX7—1H 7
Close, The. TQ4—5F 23
Close, The. TQ1—1D 26
Clovelly Rise. EX7—5D 2
Clyst Av. TQ5—5B 26
Coach Pl. TQ12—3H 9
Coach Rd. TQ12—4G 9
Coastguard Cotts. TQ1
—6D 18
Cockhaven Clo. TQ14—6G 7
Cockhaven Rd. TQ14—6G 7
Cockington La. TQ2—3F 17
Cockington La. TQ2—2F 21
Cockington Rd. TQ3—6C 16
Coffinswell La. TQ12—3H 13
Coker Av. TQ2—3E 15
Coleman Av. TQ14—3C 6
Coleridge Ct. TQ2—5F 15
Cole's Clo. TQ2—2B 28
Cole's La. TQ12—2G 13
Colin Rd. TQ3—4F 21
Collapark. TQ9—4E 29
Collaton Ct. TQ2—1F 17
Collaton Rd. TQ2—5A 14
College Rd. TQ12—4G 9
College Way. TQ6—3B 28
Colley Cres. TQ3—5D 20
Colley End Pk. TQ3—5D 20
Colley End Rd. TQ3—5B 20
Collingwood Clo. TQ1—6D 18
Collingwood Clo. TQ6—4A 28
Collingwood Rd. TQ4—6D 20
Collingwood Rd. TQ6—4A 28
Collins's Rd. TQ9—3E 29
Colwyn Ct. TQ1—4F 19
Combe La. TQ2—6F 15
Combe La. TQ5—5E 25
Combe Rd. TQ2—5G 15
Commercial Rd. EX7—4E 3
Commercial Rd. TQ4—5E 21
Common La. TQ12—4E 13
Commons La. EX7—3D 2
Commons La. TQ14—6B 6
Commons Old Rd. TQ14—6C 6
(in two parts)
Compton Pl. TQ1—4G 15
Congella Rd. TQ1—3D 18
Coniston Clo. TQ5—5B 26
Coniston Rd. TQ4—1D 22
Coniston Rd. TQ12—5E 9
Conniford La. TQ12—6A 12
Connybear La. TQ12—6E 11
Conway Cres. TQ4—6D 20
Conway Rd. TQ4—6E 21
Cooke Dri. TQ5—5C 12
Cooks Clo. TQ12—4G 5
Coombe Av. TQ14—3C 6
Coombe Clo. TQ6—3C 28
Coombe Gdns. TQ14
—4C 6
(off First Av.)

Coombe La. TQ14—3A 6
(in two parts)
Coombe Pk. Cotts. TQ1—6F 15
Coombe Pk. Rd. TQ14—3C 6
Coombe Rd. TQ3—2E 21
Coombe Rd. TQ6—3C 28
Coombe Rd. TQ14—6A 6
Coombesend Rd. TQ12—4G 5
(in two parts)
Coombeshead Rd. TQ12—1E 9
Coombe Shute. TQ9—6A 22
Coombe, The. TQ5—2E 25
Coombe, The. TQ6—3C 28
Coombe Vale Rd. TQ14—3C 6
Coombe View. TQ14—5C 6
Copland La. TQ9—3E 29
Copland Meadows. TQ9—3E 29
Copley Clo. TQ3—5C 20
Coppice, The. EX7—6D 2
Copp Path. EX7—5C 2
(off Williams Clo.)
Copythorne Clo. TQ5—3B 26
Copythorne Pk. TQ5—3B 26
Copythorne Rd. TQ5—3B 26
Corfe Cres. TQ2—1A 18
Cornacre Clo. TQ2—2F 17
Cornacre Rd. TQ2—2F 17
Cornfield Grn. TQ2
—5G 15
(off Roberts Clo.)
Corn Pk. Rd. TQ12—1B 12
Coronation Av. EX7—5D 2
Coronation Rd. TQ9—3F 29
Coronation Rd. TQ12—4F 5
(Kingsteignton)
Coronation Rd. TQ12—2F 9
(Newton Abbot)
Coronation St. TQ14—6C 6
Corsham Rd. TQ4—6D 20
Coryton Clo. EX7—4D 2
Cotmore Clo. TQ5—5B 26
Cotswold Clo. TQ2—6G 17
Country Touring Caravan Cen.
TQ12—3A 12
Courtenay Gdns. TQ12—3H 9
Courtenay Pk. Rd. TQ12
—2A 10
Courtenay Pl. TQ14
—5E 7
(off Triangle Pl.)
Courtenay Rd. TQ4—3F 23
Courtenay Rd. TQ12—3G 9
Courtenay St. TQ12—2G 9
Courtfield. TQ9—4H 29
Court Ga. Clo. TQ12—6A 12
Courtland Rd. TQ2—2E 17
Courtland Rd. TQ3—4E 21
Courtlands Rd. TQ12—3A 10
Court Rd. TQ2—4F 17
Court Rd. TQ12—1B 12
Cousens Clo. EX7—2F 3
Coverdale Rd. TQ3—5E 21
Cranford Rd. TQ3—2D 20
Crescent Ct. TQ6
—4A 28
(off Townstal Cres.)
Crescent, The. TQ12—4A 14
Cresswell Clo. TQ12—2H 13
Cresta's. TQ1—3D 18
Crest View. TQ4—6F 21
Cricketfield Rd. TQ2—2H 17
Cricket Field Rd. TQ12—1H 9
Croft Clo. TQ12—4C 8
Croft Hill. TQ2—4B 18
Croft Rd. TQ2—4B 18
Croft Rd. TQ12—4B 8
(East Ogwell)
Croft Rd. TQ12—5B 12
(Ipplepen)
Crokers Way. TQ12—5B 12
Crossgrange Trading Est. TQ12
—1A 4
Cross Hill. TQ12—2F 11
Cross La. TQ12—1G 11
Crossley Moor Rd. TQ12—3F 5
Cross Pk. TQ5—4C 26
Cross Pk. TQ9—3H 29
Cross Pk. TQ12—1G 11
Crosspark Av. TQ1—1F 17
Crossparks. TQ6—5A 28
(in two parts)
Crossway. TQ4—3F 23
Crossways Shopping Cen. TQ4
—5E 21
Crowley La. TQ9—5A 22

Crown and Anchor Way. TQ3
—5E 21
Crownhill Ct. TQ2—3H 17
Crownhill Cres. TQ2—2E 25
Crownhill Pk. TQ2—3H 17
Crownhill Rise. TQ2—3H 17
Crown Sq. TQ14—6C 6
Crowther's Hill. TQ6—2A 28
& 4C 28
Cudhill Rd. TQ5—3C 26
Culm Clo. TQ2—1E 17
Culverdale. TQ9—5H 29
Culvery Grn. TQ2—1E 17
Cumber Clo. TQ5—2C 26
Cumber Dri. TQ5—2C 26
Cumberland Grn. TQ5—2C 26
Curledge St. TQ4—6E 21
Custom Ho. Hill. TQ14—5D 6

Daccabridge Rd. TQ12—3G 13
Daccombe Hill. TQ12—3D 14
Daccombe Mill La. TQ12
—3H 13
Daddyhole Rd. TQ1—6D 18
Daggers Copse. TQ12—2E 9
Dagmar St. TQ14—6C 6
Dagra La. TQ14—6A 6
Daimonds La. TQ14—4D 6
Dainton M. TQ4—6E 21
Dairy Hill. TQ2—2F 17
Daison Cotts. TQ1—2B 18
Daison Cres. TQ1—1C 18
Dalverton Ct. TQ5—1D 26
Danby Heights Clo. TQ1—5F 19
Dane Heath Bus. Pk. TQ12
—1A 4
Danvers Rd. TQ2—5E 15
Daphne Clo. TQ1—5E 19
Darran Clo. TQ12—4G 5
Darran Rd. TQ12—4G 5
Dart Av. TQ2—1F 17
Dartington La. TQ9—2E 29
Dartmouth Rd. TQ4—2A 22
Darton Gro. TQ9—6A 22
Dart View Rd. TQ5—2E 25
Dart Vs. TQ9—5F 29
Dashpers. TQ5—4C 26
David Rd. TQ3—4D 20
Davies Av. TQ4—5D 22
Davis Av. TQ2—3G 17
Davis Ct. TQ12—1F 9
Davis Rd. TQ4—5D 22
Dawes Clo. TQ12—5E 9
Dawlish Rd. TQ14—4E 7
Dawlish St. TQ14—4E 7
Dawlish Warren Rd. EX7
—1H 3
Daws Meadow. TQ12—5F 5
Deans Clo. TQ14—5G 7
Decoy Ind. Est. TQ12—5A 10
Decoy Rd. TQ12—3A 10
Deep Dene Clo. TQ5—4B 26
Deer Pk. Av. TQ14—3C 6
Deer Pk. Clo. TQ14—3C 6
Deer Pk. Dri. TQ14—3C 6
Deerpark La. TQ14—6G 11
Deer Pk. Rd. TQ14—4A 10
Deers Leap Clo. TQ3—1E 21
Den Brook Clo. TQ1—3E 19
Denbury Rd. TQ12—6C 8
Den Cres. TQ14—5E 7
Dendy Rd. TQ4—5E 21
Den Promenade. TQ14—5E 7
Den Rd. TQ14—5E 7
Den, The. TQ14—5E 7
(in two parts)
Denys Rd. TQ1—3D 18
Denys Rd. TQ9—4F 29
Derncleugh Gdns. TQ1—1H 7
Derrell Rd. TQ4—1D 22
Derwent Rd. TQ1—2C 18
Devon Coast Country Club. TQ3
—3B 20
Devondale Chalet Pk., The. EX7
—1H 3
Devondale Ct. EX7—1H 3
Devon Sq. TQ12—2H 9
Devons Rd. TQ1—2D 18
Dickers Ter. TQ12—4F 5
Diptford Clo. TQ4—2B 22
Dixon Clo. TQ3—2B 20
Doctors Rd. TQ5—4D 26
Dolphin Ct. Rd. TQ3—2C 20
Dolphin Cres. TQ3—2C 20

Dolphin Holiday Cen. TQ5
—4E 27
Dorchester Gro. TQ2—6E 15
Dornafield Clo. TQ12—5B 12
Dornafield Dri. E. TQ12—5B 12
Dornafield Dri. W. TQ12—5B 12
Dornafield Rd. TQ12—5B 12
Dosson Gro. TQ1—2H 17
Doughy La. TQ12—6A 8
Douglas Av. TQ5—3F 27
Douglas Ho. TQ14
(off Bitton Pk. Rd.)
Dower Ct. TQ3—3F 21
Dower Rd. TQ1—2B 18
Downaway La. TQ12—1D 14
Downfield Clo. TQ5—4B 26
Drake Av. TQ2—3F 17
Drake Av. TQ14—1C 6
Drake Dri. TQ4—3D 22
Drake Rd. TQ12—2C 10
Drakes Rd. TQ4—1B 22
Drew's Field La. TQ3—2A 16
Drew St. TQ5—4D 26
Drive, The. EX7—4E 3
Drive, The. TQ5—5D 26
Drive, The. TQ14—5F 7
Drum Way. TQ12—2A 4
Duchy Av. TQ3—1D 20
Duchy Dri. TQ3—1D 20
Duchy Gdns. TQ3—6D 16
Duchy Pk. TQ3—1D 20
Dukes Clo. TQ3—5B 20
Dukes Rd. TQ9—5H 29
Duke St. TQ6—4C 28
Duncannon La. TQ9—6A 22
Dunmere Rd. TQ1—3C 18
Dunning Rd. TQ14—2C 6
Dunning Wlk. TQ14
—3C 6
(off Lake Av.)
Dunstone Clo. TQ3—2B 20
Dunstone Pk. Rd. TQ3—2B 20
Dunstone Rise. TQ3—2B 20
Durleigh Rd. TQ5—3C 26

Eagle Clo. TQ12—1E 5
Earls Ct. TQ1—3A 18
E. Cliff. TQ14—4E 7
E. Cliff Clo. EX7—3E 3
E. Cliff Gdns. EX7—3E 3
E. Cliff Rd. EX7—3E 3
E. Cliff Wlk. TQ14—4F 7
Easterfield La. TQ1—5G 15
Eastern Esplanade. TQ4 & TQ3
—6F 21
E. Pafford Av. TQ2—5G 15
East St. TQ2—3A 18
East St. TQ12—6A 8
(Denbury)
East St. TQ12—5B 12
(Ipplepen)
East St. TQ12—2G 9
(Newton Abbot)
Eastwood Cres. TQ12—1D 8
Eaton Ct. TQ14—2D 6
Ebenezer Rd. TQ3—6D 20
Eden Clo. TQ5—4D 26
Eden Gro. TQ3—4C 20
Eden Pk. TQ5—4D 26
Edenvale Rd. TQ3—2C 20
Edgelands La. TQ12—6A 12
Edgeley Rd. TQ2—5E 15
Edginswell Clo. TQ2—6B 14
Edginswell La. TQ12 & TQ2
—5G 13
Edinburgh Rd. TQ5—4E 27
Edinburgh Vs. TQ1—3A 18
Egerton Rd. TQ1—3D 18
Elba Clo. TQ4—4F 23
Elberry La. TQ4 & TQ5—6G 23
Elizabeth Av. TQ5—6B 26
Elizabeth Ct. TQ2—4A 18
Elizabeth Ct. TQ9
—4H 29
(off Furze Rd.)
Elizabeth Sq. TQ12—3C 10
Elkin's Hill. TQ5—2E 27
Ellacombe Chu. Rd. TQ1—3C 18
Ellacombe Rd. TQ1—3C 18
Ellesmere Rd. TQ1—4F 19
Elliott Gro. TQ5—3B 26
Elmbank Gdns. TQ4—6D 20
Elmbank Rd. TQ4—6D 20
Elm Dri. TQ12—4F 5

Elm Gro. TQ14—1D 6
Elm Gro. Clo. EX7—3E 3
Elm Gro. Dri. EX7—3E 3
Elm Gro. Rd. EX7—2E 3
Elmhurst Ct. TQ14—4D 6
Elmhurst Dri. TQ9—4H 29
El Monte Clo. TQ14—3D 6
Elm Pk. N. TQ3—5C 20
Elm Pk. S. TQ3—5C 20
Elm Rd. TQ5—5B 26
Elm Rd. TQ12—2H 9
Elmsleigh Pk. TQ4—6E 21
Elmsleigh Rd. TQ4—6E 21
Elm Wlk. TQ9—4H 29
Elmwood Av. TQ12—1D 8
Elmwood Cres. EX7—3E 3
Elsdale Rd. TQ4—1D 22
Embankment, The. TQ14—6B 6
Embett Hill View. TQ12—4E 9
Emblett Dri. TQ12—1D 8
Emmetts Pl. TQ12—1C 12
Empire Ct. TQ2—2B 18
Empire Rd. TQ2—2B 18
Empsons Clo. EX7—4C 2
Empsons Hill. EX7—4C 2
Enfield Rd. TQ1—2D 18
English Riviera Cen. TQ2
—5A 18
Erica Dri. TQ2—4E 15
Esplanade. TQ14—5E 7
Esplanade Ct. TQ3—5E 7
Esplanade Rd. TQ4 & TQ3
—6F 21
Eton Pl. TQ4—6E 21
Eugene Rd. TQ3—3F 21
Eveleigh Clo. TQ5—4D 26
Exe Hill. TQ2—1E 17
Exeter Av. TQ2—6E 15
Exeter Rd. EX7—4E 3
Exeter Rd. TQ12—1C 6
(Kingsteignton)
Exeter Rd. TQ12—5C 4
(Newton Abbot)
Exeter Rd. TQ14—2C 6
Exeter St. TQ14—4D 6

Factory Row. TQ2—4B 18
Fairfax Pl. TQ6—1B 28 & 4C 28
Fairfax Rd. TQ12—1A 4
Fairfield Rd. TQ12—4H 13
Fairfield Ter. TQ12—2H 9
Fairlea Clo. EX7—1F 3
Fairlea Rd. EX7—1E 3
Fair View Rd. TQ6—4B 28
Fairview Rd. TQ12—6A 8
Fairwater Clo. TQ12—4G 5
Fairway Clo. TQ5—2G 25
Falkland Dri. TQ12—3G 5
Falkland Rd. TQ2—5A 18
Falkland Way. TQ14—2C 6
Falloway Clo. TQ2—5F 15
Fallowfield Clo. TQ12—2C 10
Falmouth Clo. TQ2—1E 17
Farm Clo. TQ12—1G 13
Farmyard La. TQ3—3A 16
Farthing La. TQ3—1A 20
Farwell Rd. TQ9—4E 29
Faulkner Clo. TQ6—4A 28
Fay Rd. EX7—4E 3
Fern Clo. TQ5—3E 27
Ferncombe Clo. TQ12—1F 5
Ferncombe Dri. TQ12—1F 5
Ferndale. TQ6—4B 28
Ferndale Rd. TQ2—2E 17
Ferndale Rd. TQ14—3D 6
Fernham Ter. TQ3—4E 21
Fernicombe Rd. TQ3—4B 20
Ferrers Grn. TQ3—3H 25
Field Clo. TQ3—1E 21
Firbank Rd. EX7—1F 3
Firestone La. TQ12—6F 9
Firlands Rd. TQ2—5F 15
(in two parts)
Firleigh Rd. TQ12—2E 5
First Av. EX7—5C 2
First Av. TQ1—1B 18
First Av. TQ14—4C 6
First St. TQ3—3F 7
(off Dawlish Rd.)
First Dri. TQ14—4D 6
(off Exeter Rd.)
Fir Wlk. TQ2—1F 17

Fishchowler's La. TQ9—5E 29
Fishcombe Rd. TQ5—1C 26
Fisher Rd. TQ12—2G 9
Fisher St. TQ4—6E 21
Five Lanes Rd. TQ3—1A 20
Flavel Pl. TQ6—1B 28
Flavel St. TQ6—1A 28
Fleet St. TQ2 & TQ1—5C 18
Fletcher Clo. TQ2—2H 17
Flete Av. TQ12—3C 10
Flete Clo. TQ12—3C 10
Flood St. TQ9—5A 22
Florence Pl. TQ12—3A 10
Florida Rd. TQ1—4D 18
Flow La. TQ12—6G 7
(in two parts)
Fluder Hill. TQ12—3H 13
Fluder La. TQ12—2E 15
Fluder Rise. TQ12—4A 14
Follafield Pk. TQ5—5C 26
Football Pk. TQ3—3F 5
Footland La. TQ12—2D 14
Footlands Rd. TQ4—1D 22
Forbes Clo. TQ12—3A 4
Forde Clo. TQ12—6F 9
(Abbotskerswell)
Forde Clo. TQ12—2A 10
(Newton Abbot)
Fordens La. EX7—1G 7
Forde Pk. TQ12—3A 10
Forder La. TQ5—5F 7
(in two parts)
Forde Rd. TQ12—1A 10
Ford Rd. TQ9—3G 29
Ford Rd. TQ12—6G 9
Ford Town Clo. TQ6—4B 28
Ford Valley. TQ6—2A 28
Foredown La. TQ12—3F 13
Foresters Ter. TQ14—5D 6
Fore St. TQ1—1C 18
(in two parts)
Fore St. TQ2—4E 15
Fore St. TQ5—2D 26
Fore St. TQ6—4D 28
Fore St. TQ9—4F 29
Fore St. TQ12—5B 12
(Ipplepen)
Fore St. TQ3—5G 13
(Kingskerswell)
Fore St. TQ12—4F 5
(Kingsteignton)
Fore St. TQ14—5G 7
(Bishopsteignton)
Fore St. TQ14—4D 6
(in two parts)
Fore St. TQ14—6C 6
(Shaldon)
Forest Ridge Rd. TQ3—2C 20
Forest Rd. TQ1—3B 18
Forgeway Clo. TQ2—5G 17
Fortescue Rd. TQ3—2F 21
Foss Slip. TQ6—1A 28
Foss St. TQ6—1A 28 & 4C 28
Fouracre Way. TQ12—3G 5
Fourth Av. TQ14—3C 6
Fowey Av. TQ2—1E 17
Foxhole Rd. TQ5—5G 17
Foxhole Rd. TQ3—5B 20
Foxley Cres. TQ12—2E 9
Fox Tor Clo. TQ4—6E 23
Franeth Clo. TQ12—3F 5
Fraser Dri. TQ14—3C 6
Frederick Ter. EX7
—4D 2
(off Stockton Rd.)
Freestone Rd. TQ12—3E 5
French St. TQ14—4E 7
Freshwater Dri. TQ4—5D 22
Frobisher Grn. TQ2—3F 17
Frobisher Way. TQ4—3E 23
Froude Av. TQ2—3G 15
Fulton Clo. TQ5—5B 12
Furness Clo. TQ4—3D 22
Furrough Ct. TQ1—1D 18
Furrough Cross La. TQ1—1D 18
Furze Cap. TQ12—1E 5
Furzedown Rd. TQ12—2H 13
Furzegood. TQ3—1A 20
Furzeham Pk. TQ5—2D 26
Furzehill Rd. TQ1—3B 18
Furze La. TQ5—2E 27
Furze Rd. TQ9—4H 29

Gabwell La. TQ1—1G 15

Gainsborough Clo. TQ1—5E 19
Galloway Dri. TQ14—2B 6
Galmpton Farm Clo. TQ5
—2E 25
Galmpton Glade. TQ5—2E 25
Galmpton Holiday Pk. TQ5
—3E 25
Gard Clo. TQ2—4F 15
Garden Rd. TQ1—3C 18
Garfield Rd. TQ4—5F 21
Garlic Rea. TQ5—2E 27
(in two parts)
Garners La. TQ12—4C 8
Garrow Clo. TQ5—4D 26
Garston Av. TQ12—1G 9
Garth Rd. TQ2—5F 15
Gatehouse Clo. EX7—3D 2
Gatehouse Hill. EX7—3E 3
Gatehouse Rise. EX7—3E 3
Gate Tree Clo. TQ12—4G 5
Gattery La. TQ5—6A 26
Gaze Hill. TQ12—6A 4
George Rd. TQ2—2E 21
George St. TQ14—5E 7
Georgian Ct. TQ1—3F 19
Gerston Pl. TQ3—5E 21
Gerston Rd. TQ4—5E 21
Gestridge Rd. TQ12—3E 5
Gibson Dri. TQ4—4D 22
Gibson Gdns. TQ4—4D 22
Gibson Rd. TQ4—4D 22
Gilbert Av. TQ14—2C 6
Gilbert Clo. TQ2—3G 17
Gilbert Rd. TQ12—2B 10
Gilbert St. TQ12—2B 10
Gilbert Way. TQ4—3D 22
Gillard Rd. TQ5—3F 27
Gilpin Clo. EX7—2F 3
Gladstone Pl. TQ12—2H 9
Gladstone Ter. TQ14—4E 7
Glebeland Way. TQ2—1F 17
Glebe, The. TQ12—1A 8
Glencannock Clo. TQ1—2H 17
Glendaragh Rd. TQ14—4E 7
Glenmore Rd. TQ5—3D 26
Glen Rd. TQ3—4E 21
Glenside Clo. TQ14—3D 6
Glen, The. TQ12—3C 10
Glenthorne Clo. TQ1—5E 19
Gloucester Clo. TQ2—6E 15
Gloucester Rd. TQ12—3H 9
Gloucester Rd. TQ14—4D 6
Godfrey Av. TQ3—1E 21
Golden Clo. TQ5—5C 26
Golden Pk. Av. TQ2—4E 15
Golden Sands Holiday Pk. EX7
—1G 3
Golden Ter. EX7—4D 2
(off Brook St.)
Gollands. TQ5—2C 26
Gollands Clo. TQ5—2B 26
Golvers Hill Rd. TQ12—4F 5
Goodridge Clo. EX7—3E 3
Goodrington Holiday Cen. TQ4
—1F 23
Goodrington Rd. TQ4—4D 22
Goodstone Way. TQ4—2C 22
Gorway. TQ14—3E 7
Goshen Rd. TQ2—4H 17
Gothic Rd. TQ12—3G 9
Grafton Rd. TQ1—5C 18
Grafton Ter. TQ1—5C 18
Graham Rd. TQ3—2D 20
Grandison Av. TQ14—5H 7
Grange Av. TQ4—3E 23
Grange Clo. TQ2—4A 10
Grange Ct. Holiday Cen. TQ4
—2E 23
Grange Dri. TQ2—2D 6
Grange Heights. TQ4—3D 22
Grange Heights Clo. TQ4
—3D 22
Grange Pk. TQ14—5F 7
Grange Pk. Caravan Pk. TQ12
—1B 12
Grange Rd. TQ1—4D 18
(in two parts)
Grange Rd. TQ4—4D 22
Grange Rd. TQ12—1C 20
Grange View. TQ4—3D 22
Grange View. TQ12—1C 12
Grasmere Clo. TQ2—5G 15
Gt. Furlong. TQ4—5F 7
Gt. Gate. TQ5—3D 26
Gt. Headland Cres. TQ3—2F 21
Gt. Headland Rd. TQ3—2F 21

Gt. Hill Rd. TQ2—3E 15
Greatpark La. TQ3—5A 20
Gt. Parks Rd. TQ3—6B 20
Gt. Rea Rd. TQ5—2E 27
Gt. Tor Clo. TQ3—2C 20
Gt. Western Clo. TQ4—1E 23
Greebys, The. TQ3—5D 20
Greenaway Rd. TQ12—6E 11
(Coffinswell)
Greenaway Rd. TQ12—1F 9
(Newton Abbot)
Greenbank Av. TQ12—3C 15
Greenbank Rd. TQ5—3C 26
Greenfield Rd. TQ3—1D 20
Greenhill La. TQ12—6A 8
Greenhill Rd. TQ12—3G 13
(Kingskerswell)
Greenhill Rd. TQ12—5F 5
(Kingsteignton)
Greenhill Way. TQ12—5E 5
Greenlands Av. TQ3—5C 20
Green La. TQ5—2H 25
Greenover Clo. TQ5—4C 26
Greenover Rd. TQ5—4C 26
Green Pk. Rd. TQ3—2C 20
Green Pk. Wlk. TQ3—2C 20
Greenswood Rd. TQ5—4D 26
Green, The. TQ12—6A 8
Greenway Clo. TQ2—6F 15
Greenway Gdns. TQ2—5F 15
Greenway Pk. TQ5—5F 15
Greenway Rd. TQ1—1C 18
Greenway Rd. TQ2—5G 17
Greenway Rd. TQ5—5B 24
Grendon Ct. TQ14—4C 6
Grenville Av. TQ2—3G 17
Grenville Av. TQ14—2C 6
Grenville Clo. TQ6—4A 28
Grenville Clo. TQ12—2B 10
Grenville Way. TQ4—3E 23
Greycoat La. TQ12—4A 4
Greystone Way. TQ1—2C 18
Gropers La. TQ3—1A 16
Grosvenor Av. TQ2—6B 14
Grosvenor Clo. TQ2—6B 14
Grosvenor Rd. TQ4—6E 21
Grosvenor Ter. TQ2—6E 21
Grosvenor Ter. TQ14—3D 6
Grove Av. TQ14—4D 6
Grove Clo. TQ9—4F 29
Grove Ct. EX7—4F 3
Grove Ct. TQ14—4D 6
Grove Cres. TQ14—4D 6
Grove Gdns. TQ2—6C 14
Grove Ter. TQ14—4D 6
Grove, The. TQ4—2B 22
Grove, The. TQ9—4F 29
Guestland Rd. TQ1—2D 18
Guild Hall Yd. TQ9
—4F 29
(off Priory Ct.)
Gurneys, The. TQ3—6D 20

Haccombe Path. TQ12—3C 10
Hackney La. TQ5—5G 5
(Kingsteignton)
Hackney La. TQ12—6H 5
(Newton Abbot)
Halcyon Rd. TQ12—2G 9
Haldon Av. TQ14—3E 7
Haldon Clo. TQ1—5F 19
Haldon Clo. TQ12—3C 10
Haldon Rise. TQ12—3C 10
Haldon Rd. TQ1—5E 19
Haldon Shopping Cen. TQ1
—4C 18
Haldon Ter. EX7—4D 2
(off Hospital Hill)
Hall La. EX7—1G 7
Hall's La. TQ14—6B 6
Halsteads Rd. TQ2—5F 15
Hamelin Way. TQ3 & TQ12
—2C 16
Hamiltons, The. TQ14—6C 6
Ham La. TQ14—6B 6
Hampton Av. TQ1—1D 18
Hampton Clo. TQ1—1D 18
Hampton La. TQ1—1D 18
Hampton Rd. TQ12—2H 9
Hanover Clo. TQ5—4D 26
Happaway Clo. TQ2—5F 15
Happaway Rd. TQ2—5E 15
Harberton Clo. TQ4—2B 22
Harbourne Av. TQ4—2B 22

Harbour View Clo. TQ5—2D 26
Hardy Clo. TQ1—6E 19
Harper's Hill. TQ9—4E 29
Harpins Ct. TQ12—1H 13
Hartland Tor Clo. TQ5—5B 26
Hartley Rd. TQ4—6D 20
Hartop Rd. TQ1—6G 15
Harts Clo. TQ3—3C 6
Haslam Ct. TQ1—2B 18
Haslam Rd. TQ1—2B 18
Hatchcombe La. TQ2—5E 15
Hatcher St. EX7—4D 2
Hatfield Rd. TQ1—2B 18
Hauley Rd. TQ6—1B 28 & 4C 28
Havelock Rd. TQ1—6G 15
Haven, The. TQ14—6G 7
Hawkins Av. TQ2—2F 17
Hawkins Dri. TQ14—3D 6
Hawkins Rd. TQ12—2C 10
Hawthorn Clo. TQ12—5C 10
Hawthorn Pk. Clo. TQ2—6G 17
Haycock La. TQ5—2F 27
Hayes Clo. TQ9—5H 29
Hayes Gdns. TQ4—1D 22
Hayes Rd. TQ4—1C 22
Hayes, The. TQ5—2H 25
Hayle Av. TQ4—5E 23
Haytor Av. TQ4—3C 22
Haytor Clo. TQ14—3B 6
Haytor Dri. TQ12—2C 10
Haytor Gro. TQ12—2C 10
Haytor Ho. Caravan
Site. TQ12—4F 5
(off Crossley
Moor Rd.)
Haytor Rd. TQ1—2C 18
Haytor Ter. TQ12—2G 9
Haywain Clo. TQ2—6A 14
Hazel Av. TQ2—1F 17
Hazel Clo. TQ14—1D 6
Hazeldown Rd. TQ14—2D 6
Headland Gro. TQ3—2F 21
Headland Pk. Rd. TQ3—2F 21
Headland Rd. TQ2—1H 21
Headway Clo. TQ14—4B 6
Headway Cross Rd. TQ14
—3B 6
Headway Rise. TQ14—3B 6
Heath Ct. TQ5—2F 27
Heather Clo. TQ12—1E 9
Heather Clo. TQ14—2D 6
Heather Est. TQ12—1A 4
Heather Way. TQ5—3B 26
Heathfield Cotts. TQ12—1B 4
Heath Hill. TQ12—2B 4
Heath Pk. TQ5—2F 27
Heath Pk. TQ12—4D 10
Heath Rise. TQ5—2F 27
Heath Rd. TQ5—2E 27
Heatree Clo. TQ14—1D 6
Heaviside Clo. TQ2—4G 15
Hele Clo. TQ2—6E 15
Helens Mead Clo. TQ2—3F 15
Helens Mead Rd. TQ2—3F 15
Hele Rd. TQ2—6D 14
Hele Rd. TQ12—6E 15
Helford Dri. TQ4—5E 23
Helford Wlk. TQ4—5E 23
Hellevoetsluis Way. TQ3
—6B 16
Helmdon Rise. TQ12—1E 17
Hems Brook Ct. TQ2—1E 17
Henbury Clo. TQ1—3C 18
Hennapyn Rd. TQ2—6H 17
Hennock Rd. TQ4—3C 22
Hensford Rd. EX7—1C 2
Henty Av. EX7—3F 3
Henty Clo. EX7—2F 3
Herbert Rd. TQ2—5G 17
Hermitage Rd. TQ6—3A 28
Hermosa Gdns. TQ14—4D 6
Hermosa Rd. TQ14—4D 6
Hesketh Cres. TQ1—6E 19
Hesketh Rd. TQ1—6E 19
Hestow Rd. TQ12—1F 5
Heywood Clo. TQ4—2C 22
Heywoods Clo. TQ14
—4E 7
(off Heywoods Rd.)
Heywoods Rd. TQ14—4E 7
Highbury Rd. TQ1—3C 18
Higher Audley Av. TQ2—1A 18
Higher Brimley. TQ14—3D 6
Higher Brimley Rd. TQ14—4D 6
Higher Broad Pk. TQ6—4A 28

Higher Brook St. TQ14—4D 6
Higher Buckeridge Rd. TQ14
—2D 6
Higher Budleigh Meadow. TQ12
—2E 9
Higher Cadewell La. TQ2
—6A 14
Higher Coombe Dri. TQ14
—2C 6
Higher Copythorne. TQ5
—3B 26
Higher Downs Rd. TQ1—1D 18
Higher Dri. EX7—2F 3
Higher Edginswell La. TQ2
—2D 16
Higher Erith Rd. TQ1—5E 19
Higher Exeter Rd. TQ14—1C 6
Higher French Pk. TQ12—2E 9
Higher Furzeham Rd. TQ5
—1D 26
Higher Holcombe Clo. TQ14
—2E 7
Higher Holcombe Dri. TQ14
—1E 7
Higher Holcombe Rd. TQ14
—1E 7
Higher Kingsdown Rd. TQ14
—4B 6
Higher Lincombe Rd. TQ1
—6E 19
Higher Mnr. Rd. TQ5—2D 26
Higher Penn. TQ5—4E 27
Higher Polsham Rd. TQ3
—4E 21
Higher Queen's Ter. TQ1
—4C 18
Higher Ramshill La. TQ3
—3A 20
Higher Ranscombe Rd. TQ5
—3E 27
Higher Ringmore Rd. TQ14
—6A 6
Higher Rydons. TQ5—3B 26
Higher Sandygate. TQ12—1E 5
Higher St. TQ5—2D 26
Higher St. TQ6—1B 28 & 4C 28
(Dartmouth)
Higher St. TQ6—5D 28
(Kingswear)
Higher Union La. TQ2—4B 18
Higher Warberry Rd. TQ1
—4D 18
Higher Warborough Rd. TQ5
—1E 25
Higher Westonfields. TQ9
—4H 29
Higher Woodfield Rd. TQ1
—6D 18
Higher Woodway Rd. TQ14
—1D 6
Higher Yannon Dri. TQ14—3C 6
Highfield Clo. TQ5—3B 26
Highfield Cres. TQ3—5B 20
High Ho. Clo. EX7—3E 3
Highland Clo. TQ2—3F 17
Highland Rd. TQ2—3F 17
High St. Dawlish. EX7—4D 2
High St. Totnes. TQ9—4E 29
Highweek Clo. TQ12—6A 4
Highweek Rd. TQ12—1F 9
Highweek St. TQ12—2G 9
Highweek Village. TQ12—6A 4
Highwood Clo. TQ12—3G 9
Hillbrook Rise. TQ9—4H 29
Hillbrook Rd. TQ9—4H 29
Hilldown. TQ9—4H 29
Hiller La. TQ12—3E 11
Hillesdon Rd. TQ1—4C 18
Hillfields. TQ9—6A 22
Hillmans Rd. TQ12—3H 9
Hill Pk. Clo. TQ5—3F 27
Hill Pk. Rd. TQ1—2B 18
Hill Pk. Rd. TQ5—3F 27
Hill Pk. Rd. TQ12—1E 9
Hill Pk. Ter. TQ4—6F 21
Hillrise. TQ5—2E 25
Hill Rd. TQ12—3G 9
Hillside Clo. TQ4—4E 23
Hillside Cotts. TQ12—1B 12
Hillside Rd. TQ3—4C 20
Hillside Rd. TQ5—3D 26
Hillside Ter. TQ3
—5D 20
(off Colley End Pk.)
Hill View. EX7—1G 7

Hill View Ter. TQ1—2B 18
Hilly Gdns. Rd. TQ1—6G 15
Hilton Cres. TQ3—1F 21
Hilton Dri. TQ3—2F 21
Hilton Rd. TQ3—3H 9
Hingston Rd. TQ1—2D 18
Hodson Clo. TQ3—4C 20
Hoile La. TQ9—5A 22
Holbeam Clo. TQ12—1D 8
Holbeam La. TQ12—1A 8
Holborn Rd. TQ5—1D 26
Holcombe Down Rd. TQ14
—1D 6
Holcombe Down Rd. TQ14 & EX7
—6A 2
Hollacombe La. TQ3—2G 21
Hollam Way. TQ12—3G 5
Hollands Rd. TQ14—5E 7
Hollywater Clo. TQ1—4E 19
Holman Clo. EX7—2F 3
Holmes Rd. TQ12—2A 4
Holwell Rd. TQ5—3C 26
Holwill Tor Wlk. TQ4—2C 22
Home Clo. TQ5—4D 26
Homefield Cotts. TQ1—2E 19
Home Meadow. TQ9—4F 29
Homers Clo. TQ12—5E 5
Homers La. TQ12—5E 5
Homestead Rd. TQ1—1B 18
Homeyards, The. TQ14
—6C 6
(off Commons
Old Rd.)
Honey La. TQ12—1E 9
Honeywell. TQ12—5F 5
Honeywell Rd. TQ12—5F 5
Hoodown La. TQ6—4D 28
Hookhills Dri. TQ4—6E 23
Hookhills Gdns. TQ4—6E 23
Hookhills Gro. TQ4—6E 23
Hookhills Rd. TQ4—5E 23
Hook La. TQ5—4D 24
Hoopern Ter. EX7
—4D 2
(off Penfield Gdns.)
Hope Clo. TQ9—4H 29
Hope's Clo. TQ14—3C 6
Hope Wlk. TQ9—4H 29
(off Hope Clo.)
Hopkins La. TQ12—2H 9
Horace Rd. TQ2—5E 15
Horn Hill. TQ6—1A 28
Horns Pk. TQ14—5F 7
Horse La. TQ14—6D 6
Horsepool St. TQ5—4C 26
Horseshoe Bend. TQ4—3F 23
Hosegood Way. TQ12—4E 5
Hospital Hill. EX7—4D 2
Hound Tor Clo. TQ4—6E 23
Howard Clo. TQ2—3G 17
Howard Clo. TQ14—2C 6
Howard Ct. TQ14—2C 6
Howards Way. TQ12—1C 10
Hoxton Rd. TQ1—4C 18
Hoyle's Rd. TQ3—3B 20
Huccaby Clo. TQ5—5A 26
Humber La. TQ12—3A 6
Hunsdon Rd. TQ1—5D 18
Huntacott Way. TQ2—1E 17
Hunters Tor Dri. TQ4—6E 23
Hunterswell Rd. TQ12—2F 9
Hutchings Way. TQ14—3B 6
Hutton Rd. TQ3—2D 20
Huxner Rd. TQ12—4G 13
Huxtable Hill. TQ2—5G 17
Hyde Rd. TQ4—5E 21

Iddesleigh Ter. EX7—4E 3
Idewell Rd. TQ2—5G 15
Ilsham Clo. TQ1—4G 19
Ilsham Cres. TQ1—5G 19
Ilsham Marine Dri. TQ1—6G 19
Ilsham Rd. TQ1—4F 19
Innerbrook Rd. TQ2—4H 17
Inverteign Dri. TQ14—4B 6
Ipplepen Rd. TQ3—5A 16
Isaacs Rd. TQ2—5F 15
Ivatt Rd. TQ6—4A 28
Ivy La. TQ14—5D 6

Jack's La. TQ2—4E 15

Merrivale Clo. TQ2—3G 15
Merrylands Clo. TQ3—1E 21
Merrylands Gdns. TQ3—1E 21
Metherell Av. TQ5—4D 26
Mews, The. EX7—4E 3
Meyrick Rd. TQ1—2D 18
Middle Budleigh Meadow. TQ12
—2E 9
Middle Lincombe Rd. TQ1
—6E 19
Middle St. TQ5—2D 26
Middle St. TQ14—6C 6
Middle Warberry Rd. TQ1
—4D 18
Midvale Rd. TQ4—6E 21
Midway. TQ12—1G 13
Milber La. TQ12—3D 10
Milber Trading Est. TQ12
—3E 11
Mile End Rd. TQ12—1D 8
Milford Clo. TQ14—4C 6
Millbrook Pk. Rd. TQ2—4H 17
Millbrook Rd. TQ3—5E 21
Millbrook Vs. TQ2
—4H 17
(off Old Mill Rd.)
Mill Ct. EX7—4C 2
Mill Cres. TQ4—3A 28
Mill End. TQ12—1F 5
Mill Hill. TQ9—6A 22
Mill Hill Ct. TQ9—6A 22
Mill La. TQ2—4A 18
Mill La. TQ3—4E 21
Mill La. TQ5—6B 26
(Brixham)
Mill La. TQ5—3C 24
(Galmpton)
Mill La. TQ9—3E 29
Mill La. TQ12—4C 8
(East Ogwell)
Mill La. TQ12—6D 12
(Whilborough)
Mill La. TQ14—3B 6
Mill Leat. TQ12—2A 8
Milmans Rd. TQ3—6A 16
Milton Clo. TQ5—5C 26
Milton Cres. TQ5—5C 26
Milton Fields. TQ5—5B 26
Milton Ho. TQ12—3H 9
Milton La. TQ6—5A 28
Milton Rd. TQ1—1G 9
Milton St. TQ5—6B 26
Mincent Clo. TQ2—4F 15
Mincent Hill. TQ2—4F 15
Minden Rd. TQ14—4D 6
Minerva Bus. Pk. TQ12—2A 10
Minerva Way. TQ12—2A 10
Miranda Rd. TQ3—3C 20
Moat Hill. TQ9—5F 29
Moles La. TQ3—2C 16
Monastery Rd. TQ3—5D 20
Monksbridge Rd. TQ5—4C 26
Monterey Clo. TQ2—6H 17
Montpellier Rd. TQ1—5C 18
Moorashes. TQ9
—4F 29
(off St Katherine's
Way)
Moor Ho. TQ1—2E 7
Moore Clo. TQ12—5C 10
Moorland Av. TQ12—6A 8
Moorland Ga. TQ12—2B 4
Moorland View. TQ12—3C 10
Moor La. TQ2—4F 15
Moor La. Clo. TQ2—4F 15
Moor Pk. TQ12—1G 13
Moor Pk. Rd. TQ12—1G 13
Moors End. TQ12—4E 5
(Kingsteignton)
Moorsend. TQ12—1D 8
(Newton Abbot)
Moors Pk. TQ14—6G 7
Moorstone Leat. TQ4—4F 23
Moorview. TQ3—1A 20
Moor View Dri. TQ14—2B 6
Moor View End. TQ3—1A 20
Morgan Av. TQ2—6E 14
Morgans Quay. TQ14—6D 6
Morin Rd. TQ3—3F 21
Morningside. EX7—6C 2
Mortimer Av. TQ3—3E 21
Mote Hole. TQ12—5B 12
Mt. Boone. TQ6—3B 28

Mt. Boone Hill. TQ6—3C 28
Mt. Boone La. TQ6—1A 28
& 3B 28
Mt. Boone Way. TQ6—3B 28
Mt. Hermon Rd. TQ1—3C 18
Mt. Pleasant Clo. TQ12—4H 13
Mt. Pleasant La. TQ14—6C 6
Mt. Pleasant Rd. EX7—1G 3
Mt. Pleasant Rd. TQ1—3C 18
Mt. Pleasant Rd. TQ5—3D 26
Mt. Pleasant Rd. TQ12—4H 13
(Kingskerswell)
Mt. Pleasant Rd. TQ12—3H 9
(Newton Abbot)
Mount Rd. TQ5—3E 27
Mount, The. TQ5—1D 26
Mount, The. TQ14—3D 6
Mt. View Ter. TQ9
—4F 29
(off Grove, The)
Mudstone La. TQ5—4E 27
Mulberry Clo. TQ3—5E 21
Mulberry St. TQ14—4D 6
Murley Cres. TQ5—2F 25
Murley Grange. TQ14—5F 7
Museum Rd. TQ1—5D 18
Musket Rd. TQ12—2A 4
Myrtle Hill. TQ14—4E 7

Nash Gdns. EX7—6D 2
Nelson Clo. TQ1—6E 19
(off Rock End Av.)
Nelson Clo. TQ14—3C 6
Nelson Rd. TQ5—2D 26
Nelson Rd. TQ6—3A 28
Ness Dri. TQ14—6D 6
Ness View Rd. TQ14—1E 7
Netherleigh Rd. TQ1—2C 18
Nether Meadow. TQ3—6A 16
Netley Rd. TQ12—1G 9
Neville Rd. TQ12—1F 9
Newcomen Rd. TQ6—2B 28
& 4C 28
Newcross Pk. TQ12—2D 4
Newfoundland Way. TQ12
—2G 9
Newhay Clo. EX7—4C 2
Newhayes. TQ12—6A 12
Newhay, The. EX7—4C 2
Newlands. EX7—3E 3
(in three parts)
New Pk. Clo. TQ5—3E 27
New Pk. Cres. TQ12—3E 5
New Park Rd. TQ3—4B 20
New Pk. Rd. TQ12—3E 5
Newport St. TQ6—1A 28
& 4C 28
New Quay St. TQ14—5D 6
New Rd. TQ5—3H 25
New Rd. TQ9—6A 22
(Stoke Gabriel)
New Rd. TQ9—3G 29
(Totnes)
New Rd. TQ14—3D 6
New St. TQ3—5E 21
Newtake Mt. TQ12—3C 10
Newtake Rise. TQ12—4C 10
Newton Abbot Rd. TQ12
—3G 29
Newton Hill. TQ12—1E 15
Newton Rd. TQ12—6B 14
Newton Rd. TQ12—2A 4
(Heathfield)
Newton Rd. TQ12—2H 13
(Kingskerswell)
Newton Rd. TQ12—1H 9
(Kingsteignton)
New Wlk. TQ9—4G 29
Noelle Rd. TQ12—1D 8
Norman Clo. TQ12—1D 8
Norman Rd. TQ3—3F 21
N. Boundary Rd. TQ5—3B 26
N. Embankment. TQ6—1B 28
& 4C 28
Northernhay. TQ12—3H 9
Northfields La. TQ6—1A 28
N. Ford Rd. TQ6—1A 28
& 4B 28
N. Furzeham Rd. TQ5—1D 26
N. Hill Clo. TQ5—2C 26
Northleat Av. TQ3—6B 20
N. Lodge Clo. EX7—5C 2
N. Rocks Rd. TQ4—6E 23
North St. TQ9—3F 29

North St. TQ12—6A 8
(Denbury)
North St. TQ12—5B 12
(Ipplepen)
Northumberland Pl. TQ14
—5D 6
North View. TQ14
—6C 6
(off Commons
Old Rd.)
N. View Rd. TQ5—2E 27
Nursery Clo. TQ3—6D 20
Nursery Rd. TQ12—4F 5
Nut Bush La. TQ2—2E 17
Nuttree Orchard. TQ5—5C 26

Oak Cliff Pk. EX7—1H 3
Oak Clo. TQ12—5G 5
Oakford. TQ12—4E 5
Oak Hill. EX7—6C 2
Oak Hill Cross Rd. EX7—6B 2
Oak Hill Cross Rd. TQ14 & EX7
—2F 7
Oak Hill Rd. TQ1—3A 18
Oakland Dri. EX7—5D 2
Oakland Rd. TQ12—3B 10
Oakland Wlk. EX7—5D 2
Oak Lawn Ter. TQ1
—2A 18
(off St Vincents Rd.)
Oakley Clo. TQ14—2D 6
Oak Pk. Av. TQ2—1G 17
Oak Pk. Clo. TQ2—1G 17
Oak Pk. Rd. EX7—3E 3
Oak Pk. Rd. TQ2—1E 9
Oak Pk. Vs. EX7—3E 3
Oak Pl. TQ12—2H 9
Oaks, The. TQ12—5C 10
Oak Tree Dri. TQ12—5C 10
Oak Tree Gro. TQ14—6C 6
Oakymead Pk. TQ12—5E 5
Oatlands Dri. TQ4—1D 22
Occombe Valley Rd. TQ3
—1D 20
Ocean View Cres. TQ5—6B 26
Ocean View Dri. TQ5—6B 26
Octon Gro. TQ1—2H 17
Oddicombe Beach Hill. TQ1
—1D 18
Odlehill Gro. TQ12—1B 12
Ogwell End Rd. TQ12—4E 9
Ogwell Mill Rd. TQ12—3D 8
Ogwell Rd. TQ12—4D 8
Oke Tor Clo. TQ3—1F 21
Oldenburg Pk. TQ3—4F 21
Old Exeter Rd. TQ12—1G 9
Old Farm Way. EX7—6D 2
Old Ga. Ho. Rd. EX7—3E 3
Old Mill La. TQ6—3A 28
Old Mill Rd. TQ2—1H 21
Old Newton Rd. TQ12—1A 4
(Heathfield)
Old Newton Rd. TQ12—1F 13
(Kingskerswell)
Old Paignton Rd. TQ2—1G 21
(in two parts)
Old Quay St. TQ14—5D 6
Old Rd. TQ5—2E 25
Old Teignmouth Rd. EX7
—6D 2
Old Torquay Rd. TQ3—3F 21
Old Torwood Rd. TQ1—5D 18
Old Totnes Rd. TQ12—4F 9
Old Town St. EX7—4C 2
Oldway Rd. TQ3—4E 21
Old Widdicombe La. TQ3
—4A 20
Old Woods Hill. TQ2—2H 17
Old Woods Trading Est. TQ2
—1H 17
Orange Gro. TQ2—6F 15
Orbec Av. TQ12—4G 5
Orchard Clo. EX7—4D 2
Orchard Clo. TQ5—2E 25
(Brixham)
Orchard Clo. TQ5—2F 25
(Galmpton)
Orchard Clo. TQ12—2G 9
(East Ogwell)
Orchard Clo. TQ12—4G 5
(Kingsteignton)
Orchard Clo. TQ12—1E 5
(Sandygate)
Orchard Clo. TQ14—6B 6

Orchard Dri. TQ12—5B 12
(Ipplepen)
Orchard Dri. TQ12—3G 13
(Kingskerswell)
Orchard Gdns. EX7—4D 2
Orchard Gdns. TQ14—5E 7
Orchard Gro. TQ5—5D 26
Orchard Rd. TQ1—3C 18
Orchard Rd. TQ2—6E 15
Orchards, The. TQ5—2E 25
Orchard Ter. TQ2—3H 9
Orchard Ter. TQ12—6G 9
(Abbotskerswell)
Orchard Ter. TQ12—2G 13
(Kingskerswell)
Orchard, The. EX7—1G 7
Orchard, The. TQ14—5G 7
Orchard Way. TQ9—5A 22
Orchid Av. TQ12—4F 5
Orchid Vale. TQ12—4F 5
Orestone La. TQ12—4C 14
Orient Rd. TQ3—3G 21
Orley Rd. TQ12—6A 12
Osborn Rd. TQ3—1D 20
Osborne St. TQ12—2A 10
Osmonds La. TQ14—5D 6
Osmonds M. TQ14
—5D 6
(off Osmonds La.)
Osney Av. TQ4—1E 23
Osney Cres. TQ4—1E 23
Osney Gdns. TQ4—1E 23
Otter Rd. TQ2—2F 15
Overclose. TQ3—3B 20
Overdale Clo. TQ2—3E 15
Overgang. TQ5—2E 27
Overgang Rd. TQ5—1D 26
Oxenham Grn. TQ2—3G 17
Oxford Ct. TQ2—6E 15
Oxford La. TQ5—2B 28
Oxford St. TQ6—2B 28
Oxlea Clo. TQ1—5F 19
Oxlea Rd. TQ1—5F 19
Oyster Bend. TQ4—3F 23
Oyster Clo. TQ4—3F 23

Packhall La. TQ5—5B 26
(in two parts)
Padacre Rd. TQ2—3F 15
Paddocks, The. TQ12—6G 9
Paddons Coombe. TQ12—2F 5
Paddons La. TQ12—2C 6
(in two parts)
Pafford Av. TQ2—5G 15
Pafford Clo. TQ2—5F 15
Paige Adams Rd. TQ9—3E 29
Paignton Rd. TQ9—5A 22
Palace Av. TQ3—5E 21
(in two parts)
Palace Pl. TQ3—5E 21
Palatine Clo. TQ1—4C 18
Palermo Rd. TQ1—2D 18
Palk Clo. TQ14—6B 6
Palk St. TQ2—5C 18
Palm Rd. TQ2—4B 18
Paradise Glen. TQ14—3D 6
Paradise Pl. TQ5—2D 26
Paradise Rd. TQ14—3D 6
Paradise Wlk. TQ4—1F 23
Paris Rd. TQ2—3F 15
Park Av. TQ5—4C 26
Park Ct. TQ5—2F 27
Parkers Clo. TQ9—5G 29
Parkers Way. TQ9—4G 29
Parkfield Clo. TQ3—6A 16
Parkfield Rd. TQ9—4H 29
Parkfield Rd. TQ1—2A 18
Parkham Glade. TQ5—3D 26
Parkham La. TQ5—3D 26
(in three parts)
Parkham Rd. TQ5—3D 26
Parkham Towers. TQ5
—3D 26
(off Wren Hill)
Park Hill. TQ14—4D 6
Parkhill Rd. TQ1—6C 18
Park Hill Vs. TQ14
—5D 6
(off Park Hill)
Parkhurst Rd. TQ1—2A 18
Parkland Caravan Pk. TQ4
—4D 22
Parklands. TQ9—3F 29
(in two parts)

Orchard Dri. TQ12—5B 12
(Ipplepen)
Park La. TQ1—6C 18
Park M. TQ5—2F 27
Park Rise. EX7—5G 3
Park Rd. EX7—4D 2
Park Rd. TQ6—6G 15
Park Rd. TQ12—2G 13
Park Row Cotts. EX7
—4D 2
(off Stockton Rd.)
Parkside Rd. TQ4—5F 21
Park View. TQ12—5C 10
Parson St. TQ14—4D 6
Paternoster La. TQ12—5A 12
Pathfields. TQ9—4G 29
Pavilion, The. TQ2—6C 18
Pavor Rd. TQ2—5G 15
Peak Tor Av. TQ1—6D 18
Peaseditch. TQ5—4F 27
Peasland Rd. TQ2—3F 15
Pellew Arc. TQ14—5D 6
(off Teign St.)
Pellew Way. TQ14—2C 6
Pembroke Clo. TQ3—6B 16
Pembroke Rd. TQ1—4C 18
Pembroke Rd. TQ3—4B 20
Pencorse Rd. TQ2—1A 18
Pendennis Rd. TQ2—1A 18
Penfield Gdns. EX7—4C 2
Penn Inn Clo. TQ12—3B 10
Penn La. TQ5—4D 26
Penn Meadows. TQ5—4E 27
Pennsylvania Rd. TQ1—4C 18
Pennyacre Rd. TQ14—3E 7
Penny's Hill. TQ1—3A 18
Penpethy Clo. TQ5—3C 26
Penpethy Rd. TQ5—2C 26
Penrhyn Pl. TQ14—6C 6
Penshurst Rd. TQ12—4G 9
Pensilva Pk. TQ5—4D 26
Pentridge Av. TQ2—1F 21
Penwill Way. TQ4—1C 22
Peppery La. TQ14—6E 6
Perinville Rd. TQ1—2E 19
Perros Clo. TQ12—3B 10
Peters Cres. TQ3—6A 16
Petitor Gdns. TQ1—6G 15
Petitor Rd. TQ1—6G 15
Petitwell La. TQ1—6G 15
Picker Head Hill. TQ14—6C 6
Pidgley Rd. EX7—1F 3
Piermont Pl. EX7—4E 3
Pillar Av. TQ5—2C 26
Pillar Clo. TQ5—2C 26
Pillar Cres. TQ5—2C 26
Pilmuir Av. TQ2—4H 17
Pimlico. TQ1—4C 18
Pimm Rd. TQ3—4B 20
Pine Clo. TQ5—6C 26
Pines Rd. TQ3—3B 20
Pine View Av. TQ1—3D 18
Pine View Gdns. TQ1—3D 18
Pine View Rd. TQ1—3D 18
Pinewood Clo. EX7—2G 3
Pinewood Rd. TQ12—3B 10
Pit Hill Rd. TQ12—6A 4
Pitland La. TQ12—1D 14
Pitt La. EX7—3B 2
Plainmoor. TQ1—2C 18
Plains. TQ9—4G 29
Plantation Clo. TQ12—4C 10
Plantation Ter. EX7—4D 2
Platway La. TQ14—6B 6
Pleasant Ter. TQ3—5D 20
Plym Clo. TQ2—2E 17
Plymouth Rd. TQ9—4E 29
Polhearne La. TQ5—4C 26
Polhearne Way. TQ5—4C 26
Polsham Pk. TQ3—4E 21
Pomeroy Av. TQ5—2B 26
Pomeroy Rd. TQ12—2F 9
Poplar Clo. TQ5—6A 26
Poplar Clo. TQ12—5G 5
Poplars Dri. TQ3—1A 20
Porlock Way. TQ4—3C 22
Port Hill. TQ5—2D 24
Portland Av. TQ14—2E 7
Portland Rd. TQ1—2C 18
Potters Hill. TQ1—4C 18
Pottery Rd. TQ1—2E 7
Pound Field. TQ9—5A 22
Pound La. TQ12—3G 13
Pound La. TQ14—6A 6
(off Long La.)
Pound La. TQ14—5E 7
(off Regent St.)

Torbay 37

Poundsgate Clo. TQ5—3F 27
Powderham Rd. TQ2—6E 15
Powderham Rd. TQ12—2G 9
Powderham Ter. TQ12—3G 9
Powderham Ter. TQ12—5E 7
Preston Down Av. TQ3—1E 21
Preston Down Rd. TQ3—6B 16
Primley Clo. TQ3—6B 20
Primley Pk. TQ3—6C 20
Primley Pk. E. TQ3—6D 20
Primrose Clo. TQ12—4F 5
Prince Charles Ct. TQ2—4G 15
Prince Rupert Way. TQ12
—2B 4
Princes Rd. TQ1—4C 18
Princes Rd. E. TQ1—4D 18
Princes Rd. W. TQ1—4C 18
Princess Pde. TQ2—6C 18
Princess Rd. TQ12—3H 13
(Kingskerswell)
Princess Rd. TQ12—3E 5
(Kingsteignton)
Prince's St. EX7—4D 2
Princes St. TQ1—2E 19
Princes St. TQ3—5E 21
Prince St. TQ12—2H 9
Priory Av. TQ9—3F 29
Priory Av. TQ12—2H 13
Priory Ct. TQ9—4F 29
Priory Dri. TQ9—3F 29
Priory Gdns. EX7—4E 3
Priory Gdns. TQ9—3F 29
Priory Hill. EX7—4E 3
Priory Hill. TQ9—3F 29
Priory Pk. Rd. EX7—4D 2
Priory Rd. EX7—4E 3
Priory Rd. TQ1—1C 18
Priory Rd. TQ1—1C 12
Priory Ter. TQ9—3F 29
(off Priory Hill.)
Promenade. TQ3—3G 21
Promenade. TQ4—6G 23
(Broadsands)
Promenade. TQ12—1F 23
(Paignton)
Promenade. TQ14—5E 7
Prospect Rd. TQ5—2D 26
Prospect Ter. TQ12—2H 9
Pump St. TQ5—2E 27
Purbeck Av. TQ2—1F 21

Quantocks Rd. TQ2—6F 17
Quarry Gdns. TQ3—4D 20
Quay Rd. TQ12—2A 10
(in two parts)
Quay Ter. TQ12—2A 10
Quay, The. TQ5—2E 27
Quay, The. TQ6—1B 28 & 4C 28
(Dartmouth)
Quay, The. TQ6—5A 24
(Dittisham)
Queen Elizabeth Dri. TQ3
—5B 20
Queen La. EX7—4D 2
Queens Clo. TQ12—3G 5
Queen's Cres. TQ5—4E 27
Queen's Pk. Rd. TQ4—5F 21
Queen's Rd. TQ4—5F 21
Queen's Rd. TQ5—1D 26
Queens Ter. TQ9
—3F 29
(off Station Rd.)
Queen St. EX7—4D 2
Queen St. TQ1—4C 18
Queen St. TQ12—2H 9
Queen St. TQ14—5D 6
Queensway. TQ2—3G 17
Queensway. TQ12—3B 10
Queensway. TQ2—2H 17
Queensway Cres. TQ2—2H 17
Queensway Ho. TQ12—3B 10
Quentin Av. TQ5—5C 26
Quinta Clo. TQ1—3D 18
Quinta Ct. TQ1—2D 18
Quinta Rd. TQ1—3D 18

Radnor Ter. TQ9—3F 29
Radway Hill. TQ14—5H 7
Radway St. TQ14—5H 7
Rainbow Ct. TQ2—3G 17
Raleigh Av. TQ2—3G 17
Raleigh Clo. TQ6—4A 28

Raleigh Dri. TQ4—3E 23
Raleigh Rd. TQ12—2C 10
Raleigh Rd. TQ14—2C 6
Raleigh St. TQ6—1B 28
Ramshill Rd. TQ3—3B 20
Randolph Ct. TQ12—1F 9
Ranscombe Clo. TQ5—2F 27
Ranscombe Rd. TQ5—2C 27
Rathmore Rd. TQ2—5H 17
(in three parts)
Rawlyn Rd. TQ2—5G 17
Rea Barn Clo. TQ5—3E 27
Rea Barn Rd. TQ5—3E 27
Rea Dri. TQ5—2E 27
Rectory Rd. TQ12—4D 8
Redavon Rise. TQ2—1E 17
Red Brook Clo. TQ4—4F 23
Redburn Clo. TQ3—4D 20
Redburn Rd. TQ3—4D 20
Redcliffe Rd. TQ2—6H 15
Reddenhill Rd. TQ1—3D 18
Redgate Clo. TQ1—3E 19
Redlands Ct. TQ12—4C 20
Redoubt Hill. TQ6—4D 24
Redstart Clo. TQ12—4E 9
Redwalls Meadow. TQ6—3B 28
Redwell La. TQ3—3C 20
Redwell Rd. TQ3—3C 20
Redworth Ter. TQ9—3F 29
Reed Vale. TQ14—4C 6
Reeves Rd. TQ2—5H 17
Regent Gdns. TQ14
—5E 7
(off Regent St.)
Regent St. EX7—4D 2
Regent St. TQ14—5E 7
Reynell Av. TQ12—2C 10
Reynell Rd. TQ12—5E 9
Rhodanthe Rd. TQ3—2E 21
Richards Clo. EX7—1G 7
Richmond Clo. TQ1—4H 19
Richmond Ct. TQ3—4E 21
Richmond Hill. TQ12—2H 13
Ridge Hill. TQ6—3B 28
Ridge La. TQ3—1C 16
Ridge Rd. TQ1—1G 15
Ridge Rd. TQ12—2G 11
Ridges, The. TQ6—6A 28
Ridgeway Clo. TQ12—4C 10
Ridgeway La. TQ12—1B 14
Ridgeway Rd. TQ1—6H 19
Ridgeway Rd. TQ12—4B 10
Ridley Hill. TQ6—5D 28
Rillage La. TQ2—3A 18
Ringmore Clo. TQ14—6B 6
Ringmore Rd. TQ14—6A 6
Ringslade Clo. TQ12—6A 4
Ringslade Rd. TQ12—6A 4
Rippon Clo. TQ5—5A 26
Riverside. TQ14—6C 6
Riverside Ct. TQ12—1A 10
Riverside Rd. TQ6—4A 24
Riviera Ter. EX7—3F 3
Riviera, The. TQ4—6E 7
Robers Rd. TQ12—3E 5
Roberts Clo. TQ2—5G 15
Roberts Way. TQ12—1E 9
Rock Clo. TQ4—6F 23
Rock End Av. TQ1—6D 18
Rock Ho. La. TQ1—1H 15
Rock La. TQ14—3C 6
(in three parts)
Rock Pk. TQ6—3A 28
Rock Rd. TQ2—5C 18
Rocombe Clo. TQ2—3E 15
Rocombe Hill. TQ12—6H 11
Rodney Clo. TQ4—3E 23
Rogada Ct. TQ5—5E 27
Rooklands Av. TQ1—2A 18
Rope Wlk. TQ14—4D 6
Ropewalk Hill. TQ5—2D 26
Rose Acre Ter. TQ5—3E 27
Rose Hill. TQ12—3G 13
Rosehill Clo. TQ1—4D 18
Rosehill Gdns. TQ12—3G 13
Rosehill Rd. TQ1—4C 18
Roselands Dri. TQ4—2B 22
Roseland Sq. TQ4—1F 23
Roselands Rd. TQ4—2C 22
Rosemary Av. TQ12—1E 9
Rosemary Ct. TQ3—3E 21
Rosemary Gdns. TQ3
—3C 20
Rosery Rd. TQ4—1H 17

Roseville St. TQ6—1A 28
& 4C 28
Rosewarne Av. TQ12—3C 10
Rossall Rd. TQ3—6D 20
Rosyl Av. EX7—1G 7
Rotherfold. TQ9—4E 29
Rougemont Av. TQ2—6B 14
Roundham Av. TQ4—1G 23
Roundham Cres. TQ4—6G 21
Roundham Gdns. TQ4—1F 23
Roundham Rd. TQ4—6E 21
Roundhead Rd. TQ12—1A 4
Roundhill Rd. TQ2—1G 21
Roundings, The. TQ5—2E 25
Roundmoors Clo. TQ12—5H 13
Roundway, The. TQ12—1G 13
Rousdown Rd. TQ2—5H 17
Rowan Clo. TQ12—4E 9
Rowantree Rd. TQ12—4B 10
Rowan Way. TQ5—1C 26
Rowbrook Clo. TQ4—2B 22
Rowcroft Rd. TQ3—3F 21
Rowdens Rd. TQ2—4A 18
Rowdens, The. TQ14—3F 7
Rowley Rd. TQ1—1C 18
Rowsell's La. TQ9—4G 29
Royal Pines. TQ1—6E 18
Ruckamore Rd. TQ2—4H 17
Rundle Rd. TQ12—1H 9
Rushlade Clo. TQ4—3C 22
Rush Way. TQ9—4H 29
Russell Ct. TQ9—4F 29
(off Victoria St.)
Ryde Clo. TQ2—5F 15
Rydon Acres. TQ9—5A 22
Rydon Acres. TQ12—3F 5
Rydon Est. TQ12—3F 5
Rydon Ind. Est. TQ12—5E 5
Rydon La. TQ12—1D 12
Rydon Path. TQ12—1F 5
Rydon Rd. TQ12—2F 5
Rydons. TQ5—3B 26

Saddle, The. TQ4—3F 23
St Agnes La. TQ2—6H 17
St Albans Rd. TQ1—2D 18
St Andrews Rd. TQ4—6F 21
St Anne's Ct. TQ12—2F 9
St Anne's Rd. TQ1—2D 18
St Augustine's Clo. TQ4—4F 15
St Bartholomew Way. TQ12
—5C 8
St Catherine's Rd. TQ1—1C 18
St Clements Ct. TQ6
—3A 28
(off Church Rd.)
St David's Rd. TQ14—1D 6
St Dominicans Clo. TQ1—1C 18
St Edmund's Rd. TQ1—2C 18
(in two parts)
St Efride's Rd. TQ2—4A 18
St Georges Cres. TQ1—2D 18
St George's Rd. TQ1—2D 18
St Ives Ct. TQ1—3B 18
St James Pl. TQ1—2E 19
St James Rd. TQ1—2E 19
St James's Ho. TQ14
—4D 6
(off Fore St.)
St James's Precinct.
TQ14—4D 6
(off Bitton Pk. Rd.)
St John's Clo. TQ14—6G 7
St Johns St. TQ1—1A 10
St John's Ter. TQ9
—3E 29
(off Station Rd.)
St Katharine's Rd. TQ1—3A 18
St Katherine's M. TQ1
—4F 29
(off St Katherine's
Way)
St Katherine's Way. TQ9
—4F 29
St Leonard's Rd. TQ12—3G 9
St Luke's Clo. TQ4—4C 10
St Luke's Pk. TQ2—5B 18
St Luke's Rd. TQ2—4B 18
St Luke's Rd. TQ12—4B 10
St Luke's Rd. N. TQ2—5B 18
St Luke's Rd. S. TQ2—5B 18
St Margaret's Av. TQ1—2C 18
St Margaret's Clo. TQ1—1C 18
St Margaret's Rd. TQ1—1C 18

St Mark's Rd. TQ1—6E 19
St Marychurch Rd. TQ1—6G 15
St Marychurch Rd. TQ12
—3B 10
St Mary's Bay Holiday Cen. TQ5
—4F 27
St Mary's Clo. TQ5—5C 26
St Marys Clo. TQ12—1B 12
St Mary's Ct. TQ3—5D 20
St Mary's Ct. TQ12—3G 9
St Mary's Rd. TQ5—5D 26
St Mary's Rd. TQ12—3G 9
St Mary's Rd. TQ14—2C 6
St Mary's Sq. TQ12—4C 26
St Matthew's Rd. TQ2—5G 17
St Matthias Chu. Rd. TQ1
—4F 19
St Mawes Dri. TQ4—5E 23
St Michaels. TQ12
—3H 9
(off Courtenay Rd.)
St Michael's Clo. TQ1—3H 17
St Michael's Rd. TQ1—2H 17
St Michael's Rd. TQ2—5D 20
St Michael's Rd. TQ12—5E 5
(Kingsteignton)
St Michael's Rd. TQ12—4A 10
(Newton Abbot)
St Michael's Rd. TQ14—2E 7
St Michael's Ter. TQ1—4C 18
St Paul's Ct. TQ12—3G 9
St Paul's Cres. TQ1—2C 18
St Paul's Rd. TQ1—2C 18
St Paul's Rd. TQ3—2G 21
St Paul's Rd. TQ12—3G 9
St Peter's Hill. TQ5—2E 27
St Peter's Quay. TQ9—5G 29
St Vincent's Clo. TQ1—2A 18
St Vincent's Rd. TQ1—2A 18
Salisbury Rd. TQ2—5E 15
(in three parts)
Salisbury Rd. TQ12—1A 10
Salisbury Ter. TQ14—4E 7
Saltern Rd. TQ4—6F 21
Saltings, The. TQ14—6B 6
Salty La. TQ14—6B 6
Sanders Rd. TQ5—2B 26
Sand La. TQ9—1H 29
Sandown Rd. TQ4—3C 22
Sandpath Rd. TQ12—5F 5
Sandquay Rd. TQ6—2C 28
Sandringham Dri. TQ3
—1D 20
Sandringham Gdns. TQ3
—1E 21
Sandringham Rd. TQ12—2B 10
Sands Ct. TQ4—6E 21
Sands Rd. TQ4—6F 21
Sandygate. TQ12—2D 4
Sandygate Mill. TQ12—1E 5
Sandy La. EX7—2F 3
Sanford Rd. TQ2—4A 18
San Remo Ter. EX7—4F 3
Saturday's La. TQ12—6G 13
Sawyer Dri. TQ14—2B 6
Saxon Meadow. TQ4—6A 20
Scarborough Pl. TQ2—4A 18
Scarborough Rd. TQ2—4A 18
School Hill. EX7—4D 2
School Hill. TQ9—6A 22
School La. TQ4—1D 8
School La. TQ14—6C 6
School Rd. TQ12—2G 13
(Kingskerswell)
School Rd. TQ12—2H 9
(Newton Abbot)
Scoresby Clo. TQ2—3G 15
Sea La. TQ5—3F 27
Sea Lawn Ter. EX7
—3F 3
(off Exeter Rd.)
Seale Clo. TQ6—3A 28
(off Mill Cres.)
Seaton Clo. TQ1—2E 19
Seaview Cres. TQ3—2F 21
Seaway Clo. TQ2—6H 17
Seaway Ct. TQ2—6A 18
Seaway Ct. TQ5—3C 26
Seaway Cres. TQ3—3G 21
Seaway Gdns. TQ3—3G 21
Seaway La. TQ2—5G 17
Seaway Rd. TQ2—3F 21
Secmaton La. EX7—2E 3
Second Av. EX7—5C 2
Second Av. TQ1—1B 18
Second Av. TQ14—4C 6

Second Dri. TQ14—3F 7
(off Dawlish Rd.)
Second Dri. TQ14—4D 6
(off Yannon Dri.)
Sefton Ct. TQ1—2E 19
Sellick Av. TQ5—4E 27
Severn Rd. TQ2—2E 17
Seymour Dri. TQ2—3F 15
Seymour Pl. TQ9—4G 29
Seymour Rd. TQ12—1G 9
Shadynook Caravan Site. TQ12
—4F 5
Shakespeare Clo. TQ3—3G 17
Shaldon Bri. TQ14—5C 6
Shaldon Rd. TQ12—1H 11
(Combeinteignhead)
Shaldon Rd. TQ12—3B 10
(Newton Abbot)
Shaldon Rd. TQ14—6A 6
Shapley Tor Clo. TQ5—5B 26
Sharkham Point Caravan Pk.
TQ5—5E 27
Sharpham Dri. TQ9—5F 29
Sharpmoor Clo. TQ3—2D 20
Sharp's Clo. TQ12—2B 4
Sharp's Crest. TQ12—2B 4
Shedden Hill Rd. TQ2—5B 18
Shelley Av. TQ1—1B 18
Shelston Tor Dri. TQ4—2C 22
Shepherd's La. TQ14—1A 6
Sherborne Rd. TQ12—2G 9
Sherwell Hill. TQ2—4G 17
Sherwell La. TQ2—4G 17
Sherwell Pk. Rd. TQ2—4G 17
Sherwell Rise S. TQ2—4G 17
Sherwell Valley Rd. TQ2
—3F 17
Shillingate Clo. EX7—6C 2
Shiphay Av. TQ2—2F 17
Shiphay La. TQ2—1F 17
Shiphay Mnr. Dri. TQ2—2G 17
Shiphay Pk. Rd. TQ2—2G 17
Shirburn Rd. TQ1—2B 18
Shire Clo. TQ4—5D 22
Shobrook Hill. TQ12—1D 8
Shorland Clo. EX7—2F 3
Shorton Rd. TQ3—2D 20
(in two parts)
Shorton Valley Rd. TQ3—2D 20
Shrewsbury Av. TQ2—6F 15
Shute Hill. TQ14—5H 7
(Bishopsteignton)
Shute Hill. TQ14—4E 7
(Teignmouth)
Shute Hill Cres. TQ14—4E 7
Shute Rd. TQ9—4G 29
Shutterton Ind. Est. EX7—1F 3
Sidney Ct. EX7—4D 2
(off Old Town St.)
Sidney Wlk. TQ4—4E 23
Silver Bri. Clo. TQ4—5F 23
Silverhills Rd. TQ12—5A 10
Silver St. TQ12—6A 12
Silverwood Av. TQ12—4B 10
Singer Clo. TQ3—6D 20
Singmore Rd. TQ3—1B 20
Slade La. TQ5—2E 25
Slade La. TQ12—2C 12
Sladnor Pk. Rd. TQ1—2G 15
Sleepy La. TQ3—2D 20
Smallcombe Rd. TQ3—3B 20
Smallwell La. TQ3—1A 20
Smardon Av. TQ5—2B 26
Smardon Clo. TQ5—2B 26
Smith St. TQ6—1A 28 & 4C 28
Smith St. TQ14—5G 7
Smuggler's Caravan Pk. EX7
—1G 7
Smugglers La. EX7—1H 7
Solomon's Post Caravan and
Camp Site. TQ1—1G 15
Solsbro Rd. TQ2—5H 17
Somerset Pl. TQ9—4G 29
Somerset Pl. TQ14—5D 6
Soper Rd. TQ14—2C 6
Soper Wlk. TQ14—2C 6
Sophia Way. TQ12—3F 9
Sorrell Ct. TQ12—4E 5
South Bay Holiday Camp. TQ5
—5E 27
Southdown Av. TQ5—5C 26
Southdown Clo. TQ5—5C 26
Southdown Hill. TQ5—5C 26
Southdown Rd. TQ5—6C 26
S. Downs Rd. EX7—6D 2

S. Embankment. TQ6—2B 28
& 4C 28
Southern Clo. TQ2—3F 15
Southernhay. TQ12—3H 9
Southey Cres. TQ12—4H 13
Southey Dri. TQ12—4H 13
Southey La. TQ12—4H 13
Southfield Av. TQ3—2C 20
Southfield Clo. TQ3—3C 20
Southfield Rise. TQ3—4D 20
Southfield Rd. TQ3—4D 20
S. Ford Rd. TQ6—1A 28
& 4B 28
S. Furzeham Rd. TQ6—2D 26
S. Hill Rd. TQ1—5D 18
Southlands Rd. TQ2—4A 18
S. Parks Rd. TQ2—5E 15
South Quay. TQ4—6F 21
South Rd. TQ12—4G 9
South St. TQ2—4A 18
South St. TQ9—4F 29
Southtown. TQ6—5C 28
South View. TQ12—1C 12
South View. TQ14—5D 6
South View. TQ14
—5E 7
(off Northumberland
Pl.)
Southview Rd. TQ3—4D 20
Southway Av. TQ2—6E 15
Southwood Ct. TQ1—4D 18
Sparks Barn Rd. TQ4—1E 23
Sparrow Rd. TQ9—4E 29
Speedwell Clo. TQ5—4D 26
Spencer Rd. TQ3—5B 20
(in three parts)
Spencer Rd. TQ12—3H 9
Speranzo Gro. TQ4
—4D 6
(off Exeter St.)
Spithead. TQ6—1B 28 & 4C 28
Spring Clo. TQ12—1D 8
Springdale Clo. TQ5—5D 26
Springfield Rd. TQ1—2C 18
Springhill Rd. TQ9—4H 29
Square, The. TQ6—5D 28
Stabb Clo. TQ4—4D 22
Stabb Dri. TQ4—4D 22
Staddons Lea La. TQ2—3F 17
Stadium Dri. TQ12—5H 13
Stafford Rd. TQ4—6F 21
Stanbury Rd. TQ2—4F 15
Stanley Gdns. TQ3—4C 20
Stanley Rd. TQ1—1D 18
Stanley St. TQ4—5D 6
Stanmore Rise. TQ7—3E 3
Stanmore Tor. TQ3—6D 20
Stansfeld Av. TQ2—3A 18
Stantaway Pk. TQ1—2A 18
Stantor La. TQ3—3C 16
Stapleton Clo. TQ4—2B 22
Starpitten Gro. TQ2—4G 15
Starpitten La. W. TQ2—4F 15
Start Av. TQ14—2E 7
Station Hill. TQ5—2D 26
Station La. TQ4—5E 21
Station Rd. EX7—4E 3
Station Rd. TQ9—3F 29
Station Rd. TQ12—2A 10
Station Rd. TQ14—5E 7
Steamer Quay Rd. TQ9—4G 29
Steamer Quay Site. TQ9
—4G 29
Steartfield Rd. TQ3—4F 21
Steed Clo. TQ4—5D 22
Steep Hill. TQ1—1H 15
Stella Rd. TQ3—2D 20
Stentiford Hill Rd. TQ1—4C 18
Steppes Meadow. TQ12—3F 9
Steps La. TQ2—4G 15
(in two parts)
Stitchill Rd. TQ1—5D 18
Stockmeadow Gdns. TQ14
—6H 7
Stockton Av. EX7—4D 2
Stockton Cotts. EX7
—4D 2
(off School Hill)
Stockton Hill. EX7—4D 2
Stockton La. EX7
—4D 2
(off Stockton Rd.)
Stockton Rd. EX7—4D 2
Stoke Gabriel Rd. TQ5—1B 24
Stoke Hill. TQ9—6A 22

Stokeinteignhead Rd. TQ1
—1H 15
Stoke Rd. TQ4—2A 22
Stoneacre Clo. TQ5—4D 26
Stonelands Pk. EX7—4C 2
Stonelands Ter. EX7—4C 2
Stoneleigh Clo. TQ12—1E 9
Stoneman's Hill. TQ12—5G 9
Stone Pk. TQ4—1G 25
Stones Clo. TQ12—2F 5
Stoney Hill Rd. TQ12—4B 12
Strand. TQ1—5C 18
Strand. TQ14—6C 6
(Shaldon)
Strand. TQ14—5D 6
(Teignmouth)
Strand Hill. EX7—4E 3
Strand, The. EX7—4E 3
Strand, The. TQ5—2E 27
Strand, The. TQ14—6A 6
Strap La. TQ12—2E 5
Strawberry Ter. TQ12—3F 5
Studley Rd. TQ1—2B 18
Sturcombe Av. TQ4—2B 22
Summercourt Way. TQ5
—5A 26
Summerfield Rd. TQ2—1H 17
Summerhayes. EX7—6D 2
Summerland Av. EX7—3D 2
Summerland Clo. EX7—4D 2
Summerlands Clo. TQ5—5B 26
Summerlands Ct. TQ5—5B 26
Summer La. TQ5—4B 26
Summers Field Ct. TQ4—6F 21
Sunbury Hill. TQ1—3B 18
Sunbury Rd. TQ4—6E 21
Suncrest Clo. TQ2—5E 15
Sun La. TQ14—5D 6
Sunnybank. TQ12—1C 12
Sunny Clo. TQ12—2C 10
Sunny Hollow. TQ12—5C 8
Sunnymead Ter. TQ9
—4F 29
(off Maudlin Rd.)
Sunnyside Rd. TQ12—4H 13
Sun Valley Clo. TQ5—2D 26
Sussex Clo. TQ2—4F 15
Sutherland Clo. TQ12—5C 10
Sutherland Rd. TQ1—4D 18
Sutton Clo. EX7—3D 2
Sutton Clo. TQ3—2E 15
Swale Clo. TQ4—4D 22
Swallows Acre. EX7—3E 3
Swanborough Rd. TQ12—4C 10
Swannaton Rd. TQ6—6B 28
Swedwell Rd. TQ2—5D 14
Sweetbriar Clo. EX7—1G 7
Sweetbriar La. EX7—1G 7
Swincombe Dri. TQ3—5C 20
Sycamore Clo. TQ4—6G 23
Sycamore Way. TQ5—5B 26

Tamar Av. TQ2—2E 17
Tanners Rd. TQ4—1F 23
Tapley Gdns. TQ14—5H 7
Tarraway Rd. TQ3—2G 21
Tarr's Av. TQ12—4F 5
Tarr's La. TQ12—4F 5
Tavis Rd. TQ3—3C 20
Tavistock Pl. TQ4—5E 23
Tavy Av. TQ2—1E 17
Taylor Clo. EX7—5C 2
Teign Clo. TQ14—5F 7
Teignfield Caravan Site. TQ14
—6A 6
Teignmouth Hill. EX7—5E 3
Teignmouth Rd. EX7—6D 2
Teignmouth Rd. TQ1—2A 18
to 1H 15
Teignmouth Rd. TQ12—4G 5
Teignmouth Rd. TQ14—6H 7
(Bishopsteignton)
Teignmouth Rd. TQ14 & EX7
—2F 7
(Teignmouth & Holcombe)
Teign Rd. TQ12—2A 10
Teign St. TQ12—5A 10
Teign View Pl. TQ14—5D 6
Teignview Rd. TQ14—5D 6
Temperance Pl. TQ5
—2E 27
(off King St.)
Temperance St. TQ2—4B 18
Templer Rd. TQ3—6D 16

Templer's Rd. TQ12—1A 10
Templer's Way. TQ12—2E 5
Tennyson Clo. TQ1—1B 18
Terrace, The. TQ1—5C 18
Thatcher Av. TQ1—6G 19
Thatcher Dri. TQ14—1E 7
Third Av. EX7—5D 2
Third Av. TQ1—1B 18
Third Av. TQ14—4C 6
Third Dri. TQ14—4D 6
Thomas Newcombe Ct.
TQ6—4A 28
(off Ivatt Rd.)
Thorncliff Clo. TQ1—4F 19
Thorn Clo. TQ12—1D 8
Thorne Pk. Rd. TQ2—4G 17
Thornley Dri. TQ1—4C 6
Thrushel Clo. TQ5—5B 26
Thurlestone Gdns. TQ6—4B 28
Thurlow Hill. TQ1—3B 18
Thurlow Pk. TQ1—3B 18
Thurlow Rd. TQ1—3B 18
Ticklemore St. TQ9—4F 29
Times M. TQ9—4F 29
(off Victoria St.)
Tintagel Clo. TQ2—1A 18
Titchfield Gdns. TQ3—4C 20
Top Cliff Rd. TQ14—6B 6
(in two parts)
Torbay Clo. TQ5—2F 27
Torbay Holiday Chalets. TQ5
—1C 26
Torbay Rd. TQ2—2G 21
Torbay Rd. TQ4—5F 21
Tor Church Rd. TQ2—4A 18
Tor Clo. TQ4—6E 23
Tor Gdns. TQ12—4C 8
Tor Hill Rd. TQ2—4A 18
Tor Pk. Rd. TQ2—3A 18
Tor Pk. Rd. TQ4—2A 22
Torquay Holiday Village. TQ4
—4C 14
Torquay Rd. TQ3—5E 21
Torquay Rd. TQ12—3H 13
(Kingskerswell)
Torquay Rd. TQ12—2H 9
(Newton Abbot)
Torquay Rd. TQ14—6C 6
Torridge Av. TQ2—2E 17
Tors, The. TQ12—3G 13
Tor Vale. TQ1—3A 18
Tor View Av. TQ12—3C 10
Tor View Gdns. TQ3—5D 20
Torwood Clo. TQ1—6D 18
Torwood Ct. TQ1—5E 19
Torwood Gdns. Rd. TQ1
—6D 18
Torwood Mt. TQ1—5E 19
Torwood St. TQ1—6C 18
Tothill Ct. TQ14—6C 6
Totnes Down Hill. TQ9
—5F 29
Totnes Rd. TQ2—6D 16
Totnes Rd. TQ3—2A 20
(Marldon)
Totnes Rd. TQ4 & TQ3—6A 20
(Paignton)
Totnes Rd. TQ12—6B 12
(Ipplepen)
Totnes Rd. TQ12—4A 12
(Newton Abbot)
Tower Rd. TQ3—5E 21
Town Cotts. TQ12—1C 12
Townsend Hill. TQ12—5A 12
Townstal Cres. TQ6—4A 28
Townstal Hill. TQ6—4B 28
Townstal Pathfields. TQ6
—4A 28
Townstal Rd. TQ6—4A 28
Town Tree Hill. TQ7—4D 2
Treefields. TQ5—3C 26
Treesdale Clo. TQ3—5C 20
Trematon Av. TQ2—1H 17
Treston Clo. EX7—3E 3
Trevenn Dri. TQ12—4H 13
Triangle. TQ14—5E 7
Triangle, The. TQ14—5E 7
Trinity Hill. TQ1—6D 18
Trumans Pl. EX7—4E 3
Trumlands Rd. TQ1—6F 15
Truro Av. TQ2—6F 15
Tudor Clo. TQ4—3D 22
Tudor Rd. TQ12—2G 9
Tweenways. TQ12—4E 5
Twickenham Rd. TQ12—3C 10

Two Acre Clo. TQ3—5B 20

Undercliff. TQ6—3C 28
Underhill Rd. TQ2—6H 17
Underidge Clo. TQ3—5B 20
Underidge Dri. TQ3—5B 20
Underidge Rd. TQ3—5B 20
Under Way. TQ12—1H 13
Underwood Clo. EX7—6D 2
Union St. TQ5—2D 26
Union St. TQ2 & TQ1—3A 18
Union St. TQ6—1A 28
Union St. TQ2—2G 9
Uplands Rd. TQ3—1D 20
Up. Braddons Hill Rd. TQ1
—5D 18
Up. Cockington La. TQ2—3F 17
Up. Headland Pk. Rd. TQ3
—2F 21
Up. Hermosa Rd. TQ14—4D 6
Up. Longlands. EX7—3C 2
Up. Manor Rd. TQ3—3E 21
Up. Morin Rd. TQ3—4F 21
Up. Penns Rd. TQ3—2F 21
Upton Hill. TQ3—3B 18
Upton Hill Rd. TQ5—5D 26
Upton Mnr. Pk. TQ5—5D 26
Upton Mnr. Rd. TQ5—5C 26
Upton Rd. TQ1—3A 18

Vale Clo. TQ5—2E 25
Vale Rd. TQ12—2H 13
(Kingswell)
Vale Rd. TQ12—4A 10
(Newton Abbot)
Valletort Clo. TQ5—3B 26
Valletort Pk. TQ5—3B 26
Valley Clo. TQ14—2B 6
Valley Pl. TQ12—1D 8
Valley View Clo. TQ1
—2A 18
Vanehill Rd. TQ1—6D 18
Vansittart Rd. TQ2—3A 18
Vaughan Pde. TQ2—6C 18
Vaughan Rd. TQ2—6C 18
Vavasours Slip. TQ6—3C 28
Veille La. TQ12—1F 17
Velland Av. TQ2—1E 17
Venford Clo. TQ4—5E 23
Verbena Ter. TQ14—6B 6
Vernon Clo. TQ1—6D 18
Vicarage Clo. TQ5—2D 26
Vicarage Clo. TQ6—6A 22
Vicarage Gdns. EX7—4C 2
Vicarage Gro. TQ9—5A 22
Vicarage Hill. TQ2—5F 17
Vicarage Hill. TQ3—6A 16
Vicarage Hill. TQ5—2D 26
Vicarage Hill. TQ6—1A 28
& 4B 28
Vicarage Rd. TQ12—4F 5
Vicarage Rd. TQ2—5G 17
Vicarage Rd. TQ3—1B 20
Vicarage Rd. TQ5—4D 26
Vicarage Rd. TQ9—5A 22
Vicarage Rd. TQ12—1C 12
Victoria Pde. TQ1—6C 18
Victoria Pk. Rd. TQ1—2C 18
Victoria Pl. TQ2—2H 9
Victoria Rd. TQ1—3E 18
Victoria Rd. TQ5—1G 27
Victoria Rd. TQ6—1A 28
& 4A 28
Victoria Shopping Cen. TQ4
—5F 21
Victoria St. TQ6—4A 28
Victoria St. TQ9—4F 29
Victoria Ter. TQ12—4F 5
Victoria Ter. TQ14
—6C 6
(off Bridge Rd.)
Victory Rd. TQ6—4A 28
Villiers Av. TQ12—3C 10
Vine Rd. TQ2—3A 18
Vinery, The. TQ1
—5C 18
(off Montpellier Rd.)
Vittery Clo. TQ5—2C 26

Waddeton Clo. TQ4—4C 22
Waddeton Ind. Est. TQ4—3B 22

Waddeton Rd. TQ9, TQ5 & TQ4
—1A 24 & 5C 22
(in three parts)
Wain La. TQ12—1F 9
(in two parts)
Waldon Ct. TQ2—5C 18
(off St Lukes Rd. S.)
Walkham Rise. TQ2—1E 17
Wallace Av. EX7—3E 3
Wallace Av. TQ2—1F 17
Wallis Gro. TQ4—5H 7
Wall Pk. Clo. TQ5—2F 27
Wall Pk. Holiday Cen. TQ5
—2G 27
Wall Pk. Rd. TQ5—2F 27
Walls Hill Rd. TQ1—2E 19
Walnut Rd. TQ2—5H 17
Waltham Rd. TQ12—2F 9
Warberry Rd. W. TQ1—4C 18
(in two parts)
Warberry Vale. TQ1—3C 18
Warborough Rd. TQ5—1F 25
Warbro Ct. TQ1—2C 18
Warbro Rd. TQ1—2C 18
Ware Barton Caravan Site.
TQ12—5H 5
Ware Clo. TQ12—4G 5
Warecroft Rd. TQ12—4G 5
Warecross Gdns. TQ12—4G 5
Warefield Rd. TQ3—4F 21
Warfleet Rd. TQ6—5D 28
Warland. TQ9—4F 29
Warren Hill. TQ2—5C 18
Warren Rd. TQ2—5B 18
Warren, The. TQ12—2E 9
Warwick Clo. TQ1—2F 19
Washbourne Clo. TQ5—2F 27
Washington Clo. TQ3—2E 21
Watcombe Beach Rd. TQ1
—4H 15
Watcombe Heights Rd. TQ1
—3G 15
Water La. TQ2—1F 17
Water La. TQ12—3H 13
(Kingskerswell)
Water La. TQ12—1E 9
(Newton Abbot)
Waterleat Av. TQ3—6B 20
Waterleat Clo. TQ3—6C 20
Waterleat Rd. TQ3—6B 20
Waterloo Rd. TQ1—3C 18
Waterloo St. TQ14—5E 7
Waterpool Rd. TQ6—2A 28
& 5A 28
Waterside. TQ9—4G 29
Waterside Holiday Camp. TQ4
—4F 23
Waterside Rd. TQ4—4F 23
Waterwell La. TQ12—5E 11
Waverley Rd. TQ12—1G 9
Wayside. TQ5—3B 26
Wayside Rd. TQ5—3B 26
Weaver Ct. TQ2—1E 17
Weavers Way. TQ12—3G 13
Webber Clo. TQ12—5E 9
Weech Clo. EX7—4C 2
Weech Rd. EX7—4C 2
Weeke Rd. TQ6—6C 28
Week La. EX7—1F 3
Weeksland Rd. TQ2—3F 17
Weirfields. TQ9—3F 29
Wellesley Rd. TQ1—3C 18
Wellington Pl. TQ1—4C 18
Wellington Rd. TQ1—4C 18
Wellington St. TQ14—5E 7
Well St. TQ3—5D 20
Wellswood Av. TQ1—4E 19
(in two parts)
Wellswood Gdns. TQ1—4F 19
Wellswood Rd. TQ1—4F 19
Wellswood Path. TQ1—4E 19
Wembury Dri. TQ2—5G 15
Wentworth Rd. TQ12—2A 4
Wesley Clo. TQ2—4F 15
Wesley Ct. TQ2—4F 15
Wesley View. TQ12—5B 12
Westbourne Rd. TQ1—2B 18
W. Brook Av. TQ1—4C 18
W. Buckeridge. TQ14—3D 6
Westcliff. EX7—4E 3
(off Teignmouth Hill)
W. Cliff Clo. EX7—5D 2
W. Cliff Pk. Dri. EX7—5D 2
W. Cliff Rd. EX7—4C 2
Westerland La. TQ3—1A 20

TOURIST INFORMATION INDEX